MW00654472

Having lost his beloved wife and life partner several years ago, John travels inward through what he calls "several lifetimes", while he grieves and explores who he is and has become, all leading towards discovering the liberating experience of unconditional self-love. If you are in search of self-understanding and a deep appreciation of who you are, this book is for you. –Judy Dubin, author of *Fired for Success, Courageous Conversations®*

If you think you understand unconditional love, you might want to read this book as it is so much more than I thought. John's journeys through life allows the reader to experience love from many perspectives with self-love being the state that allows one to truly move forward to experience all life has to offer. –Sharon Fiehler, Founder ABC to CEO

In *The Lifetimes of a Journey* John Davis describes how grieving a river of tears taught him to accept all that life offers, to love without conditions, and to swim in an ocean of unconditional love. This is a wonderful, inspiring story. Highly recommended. –Robert J. Tallon, author of *The Enneagram Connection* and Awareness to Action

John's subtitle, "My Amazing Journey of Coming Alive and the Power of Unconditional Love" is what this book is about. Buckle up to take the journey with John as he shares his thoughts, ideas and feelings that bubbled up from his life experiences, his pain in those experiences and the lessons learned from each of those experiences. If you want a model of how to think about your life, your gifts, your experiences, your future, this is the book for you. I believe it is a must read for all who seek to find and give unconditional love. –Laura Herring, author of *No Fear Allowed*

John Davis has written an amazing book, especially for anyone who has experienced many ups and downs in their life and is looking for a guide to help them learn from their own journey through life. John leads the reader through the loss and loves of his life and how he used each one as an opportunity to learn unconditional love for himself and others. –Mike Snider, author of *STAR Leadership* and *Seeking the Light*

Your book is amazing! It's so real with raw emotions - and I am not afraid to tell you it brought genuine tears in places. Clearly written from the heart, and your journey will resonate with so many. –Wendy Haan

"I think about my mission of creating a world of unconditional love and my own life being filled with it."

The author's happy childhood—what he calls his first lifetime—ended abruptly with the death of his father, with whom his relationship had become strained, when he was a freshman in college. What he calls his second lifetime began his sophomore year of college, included the start of his engineering career and the births of his son and daughter. It ended when his first marriage broke down. His third lifetime began when he met his second wife, Kathy, in 1997 and ended when she died of pervasive cancer nearly nineteen years later in July of 2016. His fourth lifetime, he asserts, began thirteen months after her death when his grief softened into treasured memories, and he resolved to create a world of unconditional love, including self-love. This fourth lifetime, which features coaching others in the art of unconditional self-love, continues today.

Refreshingly, Davis humbly admits his mistakes and challenges along the path to unconditional love and acceptance of self and others. He takes responsibility for his contribution to the conflict he had with his father as a teenager, admits that he was largely an absentee parent, and writes nothing uncomplimentary about his first wife, the mother of his children. He decries the racist teachings of his grandparents and his parents' intolerance of religious practices different from their own, citing those as examples of conditional love he encountered in his youth. At the same time, he refrains from cloaking his successes in false modesty. He describes his rapid advance, while a young husband and father, through the ranks of his chosen field of endeavor. He tells of frequent intercontinental travel and exposure to diverse world cultures. Those who wish to achieve self-acceptance and explore masculine sensitivity may gravitate to this insightful self-help memoir. –Heather Brooks, *US Review of Books*

Leadership coach John S. Davis shares the lessons he's learned about emotional-awareness and the power of unconditional love during various stages in his *THE LIFETIMES OF A JOURNEY.* It's clear that the process of writing *THE LIFETIMES OF A JOURNEY* has been cathartic for Davis . . . it ultimately feels more like . . . a journal . . . meant for a broader audience. *–IndieReader Review*

Davis's memoir—a reflective account of love, loss, and growth that edges into heartfelt self-help—is aimed toward readers eager to "look for the possibility of unconditional love in each day." Davis believes "it is the relationship with self that sets the tone for every other relationship in our lives," a conviction he demonstrates by sharing and exploring his own relationships, especially with Kathy, his beloved late wife. Davis has divided his story into four separate "lifetimes," stretching back to childhood and covering marriage, divorce, loss, and his discovery of higher consciousness in his forties, all to examine what he has learned at each stage on that path toward unconditional self-love.

Perhaps fittingly for a book about unconditional self-love, Davis's journey reads at times something like a love letter to his development as a fulfilled and spiritual person. Davis suggests that readers seeking similar fulfillment devote great mental energy and extensive time alone to their own development. Readers new to the concept of unconditional self-love will find his definitions helpful: he differentiates between "sense of self," "confidence," and "self-love," pointing out that despite only slight differences, precision is crucial when analyzing how "self-love" has changed one's life. Still, his case might be more persuasive if it more clearly addressed the possibilities of selfishness and self involvement, how these practices fit among other life responsibilities (family, career), or issues of privilege that may impede some readers' opportunities to pursue unconditional self-love.

But this is one man's journey, offered as a source of inspiration, to find the spiritual fulfillment that best suits him. Davis describes fluidly what he has learned from childhood, his departure from constructed religion, young adulthood, and his experience of intense grief. He concludes with concise depictions of how he chooses to interact with the world, lending a framework to readers to build upon themselves. What shines through: Davis has shaped this impassioned guide to introduce others to the possibility of love without conditions.

Takeaway: One man's journey through love, loss, and spiritual fulfillment–and how to find unconditional self-love.

Great for fans of: Shannon Kaiser's *The Self-Love Experiment,* Vex King's *Good Vibes, Good Life.*
–BookLife Review, *Publishers Weekly*

the Lifetimes *of a* Journey

the Lifetimes *of a* Journey

My Amazing Journey of
Coming Alive and the Power of
Unconditional Self-Love

John S. Davis

W. Brand Publishing
NASHVILLE, TENNESSEE

j.brand@wbrandpub.com

W. Brand Publishing

www.wbrandpub.com

Cover design by JuLee Brand / designchik.net

Cover photo credit: S_Photo

Journal cover artwork: Jaxon Wesley Davis - ©2021

The Lifetimes of a Journey / John S. Davis —1st ed.

Available in Paperback, Kindle, and eBook formats.

Hardcover ISBN: 978-1-950385-77-5

Paperback ISBN: 978-1-950385-70-6

eBook ISBN: 978-1-950385-71-3

Library of Congress Control Number: 2021912172

Contents

• DEDICATION •

This book is dedicated to my Grands.

My granddaughters Nadianna and Rosemary.

My grandsons Jaden and Jaxon and

great granddaughter Lillith.

My words that follow reflect the world

I feel certain they can find.

They have my unconditional love always.

The artwork found in this book are original drawings for this project by Rosemary and Jaxon.

• INTRODUCTION •

The Lifetimes of a Journey is truly about the journey of a lifetime . . .

As I consider, examine, and reflect on my lifetime journey so far, I feel such gratitude, blessing and this compelling sense of wonder. I've been living my ordinary life, yet I feel like I am in this extraordinary place. Right now, right here. It humbles me, it excites me, it draws me into a feeling of possibility.

I feel touched by Grace as I hold that possibility. I feel so thankful knowing I have come to this place.

I am choosing to look for the possibility of unconditional love in each day, in myself, and in each of those I encounter. I sense that possibility for myself and I sense that possibility for each of us.

I believe that it IS possible to live every day in the consciousness that is experienced as unconditional love. Join me in this exploration and see what you find possible!

Original artwork by granddaughter

Rosemary Renee' Davis - ©2021

WHAT JOURNEY IS THIS?

When I started writing, I thought this book was to be a reflection on the life that I shared with my late wife, Kathy. As I've worked with my experience of that unbelievable life we had together, of unexpectedly losing her, and of the movement through my grieving process, a different focus emerged.

I began to see my life as four distinct lifetimes, each with its own profound experience of love, loss, grief, and inevitably a renewal, leading to the next "life." Each lifetime has also brought new awareness that has led to deeper levels of consciousness and a greater understanding of the power of unconditional love, and particularly of unconditional self-love.

That is the focus where I find myself today.

What I mean by unconditional love is first, a love that lets me accept myself just as I am and accept another just as they are. It's a love that does not require them or me to be a certain way, rather it encourages them to just be themselves, just as it encourages me to just be myself. It encourages us to be our completely authentic selves. In addition, it is a love that is non-judgmental, that brings compassion into the world, and that recognizes that we are all connected. Understanding our connectedness can change how we see and interact with one another in such a powerful way. I have found, it is through this realization, that the idea of unconditionally loving each other becomes possible.

If you're someone who has never experienced unconditional love, this book may present ideas and experiences that at first seem out of touch and out of reach. My hope is in reading this, you find that part of you that is capable of loving yourself . . . and even loving yourself unconditionally. I believe that it is the relationship with self that sets the tone for every other relationship in our lives.

And if you're someone who has been fortunate to have experienced a relationship of unconditional love of yourself or with another, then my hope is this book will help amplify the gift that love has brought to your life and your ability to share it with the world.

FOUR LIFETIMES OF LOVE, LOSS, AND DISCOVERY

My experience with unconditional love has included finding it, losing it, grieving over it, searching again for it and ultimately discovering that I've had it within me all the time. I believe that each of us have it in us all the time, although it just may be out of sight.

LIFETIME #1 took me from birth up through my first year of college, when my father died.

LIFETIME #2 involved the completion of college and graduate school, getting married, having kids, focusing on a career and starting to travel the world. This lifetime was over when the marriage ended in divorce.

LIFETIME #3 began when I met Kathy and encompassed the amazing life that we created together. In that lifetime, I discovered quickly what unconditional love can bring into a life – what it brought into my life. From the beginning and throughout our time together, Kathy kept encouraging me to "just be who you are." Her love was truly unconditional, and she helped me learn how mine could be as well—for her and for myself. That lifetime abruptly ended when Kathy died from breast cancer less than two years after being diagnosed.

Next was a year of grief work that I am calling my LIFETIME #3.5. During that transitional year I started writing for myself to help move through the grief. My Open Heart blog[1] became one important way of processing, dealing with, and emerging from that devastating loss.

My LIFETIME #4 is in progress and it is finding clarity now. This fourth life is emerging, even as I write this. I can now see that I have - and have been given - the chance of a lifetime. There was a time when I could not have imagined it would be possible for me to say that. It is calling me into a grand possibility that I would have

1 www.myopenheart.blog

never thought possible, especially after losing a life partner. And I sit here excited, exhilarated and really open to this new life, in a way that feels very empowering.

While I will speak to the journey through my past experiences, it is where I am at present that is the real story. I want to be able to explain the significance of where I am today. It is in this place that I find myself truly coming alive.

CONSCIOUSLY CREATING A NEW LIFE

My lifetime #3 with Kathy was so big, so beautiful, and so bountiful. We had quite the amazing love story and initially, my goal was to honor that story through my writing. But as I worked through the formative writing process, I came to realize that the real value that I can offer to others in my writing is about moving through my grief (Lifetime #3.5) and my ongoing process of rebuilding (Lifetime #4).

What I really want my story to be about is what can happen when I consciously create my life, when I get even more deliberate about living an intentional mission.

My life is truly about where I am now, what that means and what has brought me to this place.

I have found a deep desire to explore what it means to literally manifest a life that is consciously evolving from my playing with the potential in every facet of my life: health, work, relationships, finances, travel, and discretionary time. I feel empowered to evolve each facet consciously--and evolve my consciousness at the same time.

I believe that empowerment has become possible as I have explored my journey with and gained a deeper appreciation of unconditional love. The empowerment comes from my on-going evolution and understanding of my own level of consciousness.

HIGHER CONSCIOUSNESS

I WILL ALSO ADMIT that I have a very clear sense of possibility for what the future holds, both for myself and for all of us collectively. A real motivation for me to share any of this, is around my belief and my hope, that we are collectively moving to a new level of awareness in our consciousness, a level of consciousness that embodies compassion, unconditional love and a sense of our oneness.

It was in my Lifetime #2 that I began my process of waking up spiritually. In those early adult years, I started down the path of personal growth, emotional awareness and spiritual seeking. It was a very explosive time of new understanding and new experiences for me. Once I had started this phase, there was no turning back and that seeking, and exploration continues today.

I came to an awareness that the current state of affairs in the human condition – our intolerance of difference, fear of different belief systems, hatred of others not like us, killing each other over religion or resources and all the wars in general – was not going to change until (and unless) we developed a higher level of collective consciousness. It was my version of Albert Einstein's quote, "No problem can be solved from the same level of consciousness that created it."

To find that different level, it became clear to me that we would have to see each other and all that we are up to, in a completely different way, through a completely different lens. That lens would enable each of us to realize we are all connected at a spiritual level – the level where we all have that spark of the Divine within us – and that we are all in this together. Realizing that connection, realizing we are all the same at the soul level, understanding that our Essence is unconditional love, we can then shift to treat each other in a completely different way. We can treat each other with compassion, with unconditional love, and a knowing that such a world enables a completely different experience for each and all of us.

This entire path of discovery around my desire to see us living together from a place of higher consciousness clarified a central theme and vision for my life. A vision that became apparent at a critical time in my life.

I was in my forties when I began uncovering these realizations and understandings for and about myself. In sharing about my lifetimes, I hope to bring perspective on how my experiences brought me to that point and more importantly, carried me forward from that point.

I want to share how my experiences with unconditional love–and without it–have shaped me and brought me to the possibility that we can shift our collective consciousness. I want to discuss how my own consciousness has evolved through each of my lifetimes and how now, in my 4th lifetime, I am able to see and sense the emergence of a world filled with unconditional love.

I don't mean the world is there today, by any stretch of the imagination, rather that it is moving (quickly I believe) toward that point. Even given the total chaos we experience everyday around us, in so many ways, on so many levels and for so many reasons. Yes, I may be dreaming... and I know there are many others out there that envision this type of world as well.

I know it all sounds so idealistic, so ethereal, so out of reach, so unrealistic given everything we have to face in our world today. Yet, what if we could get there? What if we were capable of making such a shift in our collective consciousness?

This last question has always been a compelling question for me. So much so that I began wondering what I could do to help us get there collectively. What could I DO to help us find that way to BE? This question points me to a very daunting task, one that has no clear, easy answer. The more I have pondered on it, journaled on it, meditated on it, the more I keep coming back to one approach: my answer is how I show up in my world every day. What I can do is be, engage, and work with others in a way that honors the collective shift that I want to happen.

Back to Einstein. He also said, "The only source of knowledge is experience." I have nothing but experience (and an occasional opinion!) to share and perhaps along the way in sharing it, I can pull out some useful knowledge. I know I am finding awareness of some new knowledge for myself; you can decide if it offers any for you.

If I can make some sense out of my experiences and bring some understanding to my own evolution of consciousness, my hope is to show you that in fact, we can get to this new place and create this new world for ourselves and those who follow. This will enable the possibility to live more in that place of unconditional love, if we will make that choice. I have made my choice and I trust you will understand how and why, as you read what follows.

Original heartwork by grandson Jaxon Wesley Davis - ©2021

Lifetime #1- The Road to Conditional Love

Lifetime #1 was full of the love of family and of being a kid growing up in a loving household. There was (almost) always the joy of being with extended family, especially summers on my grandparents' farm. Childhood friendships brought delight in building forts, playing baseball and taking bicycle rides.

This lifetime was shattered when my father died. I was a freshman in college, my sisters were teenagers, and my brother was only eleven. Dad's death created all kinds of turmoil as my family struggled in its grief. I found myself propelled through this time of loss by the very strong work ethic that my father and grandfather had instilled in me. I started doing–a lot–to try to get through the grief and get my life back in order again.

I was to learn later just how much of this lifetime was defined by conditional love.

Original artwork by Rosemary Renee' Davis - ©2021

• CHAPTER 1 •

GROWING UP

One of my favorite boyhood photos is of me at about 5 years old, sitting with the best of posture on the living room couch on a Sunday morning before church next to my father, both of us wearing our bow ties. I also cherish the picture of my first day of kindergarten with my hair all "slicked-back", decked out in a light brown plaid suit, newly polished black shoes, and wearing that same bow tie. Now who wears a suit and bow tie to their first day of kindergarten? I mean, really!

It took me years to admit the pride I have in seeing myself dressed-up like that. The story I always told myself was that I had to have been the only kid dressed in a suit and tie for the first day of school. While I don't remember the exact experience, I was sure I must have been totally embarrassed. When I did let go of that apparent resentment, I realized that kindergarten moment led in part to my always wanting to dress well and I now see how that became an early awareness of loving myself. I don't recall ever challenging my mom on why she decided I had to wear that outfit. But I knew that mom loved me.

The Sunday picture of me and my dad has been a source of deepening connection with my father year after year. I look at it often and try to remember those earliest days with him. I do remember how he got me started playing baseball and the times we played catch out in the yard. He showed me how to take care of my glove by keeping it oiled and how to shape it, by wrapping it with a ball inside to form a deeper pocket to help me catch better. I knew my dad really loved me.

We were living outside of St. Louis in a little town in Illinois when I was in third grade and my baseball team won our little league championship. I can recall seeing dad smiling as our team boarded the bus, along with several of the older championship teams, to go to St. Louis to see a Cardinals baseball game. It was our reward for winning. The cool part was that we were recognized in front of a packed Sportsman Park stadium by getting to go onto the field when they called our team's name. I kept the souvenir pennant from that game on my bedroom wall for a long time. It was the best world of a kid just having fun. I not only felt my dad's pride around that baseball accomplishment, but I also felt it for myself. I felt his love and it let me feel how to love myself.

There was another third-grade moment, which was not any fun at all, that stuck with me a long, long time. I was bullied in the bathroom by a group of sixth graders, just because I was a little kid, and they were bigger. There was a moment of being scared and that fear anchored itself deeply in my psyche—so much so that I found myself looking over my shoulder that year, every time I went into the bathroom. It was years later that I was finally able to see the dynamics more clearly and have some compassion for myself and for those other boys. That experience taught me about standing up for myself and what it was like to handle stressful moments. It was a moment of learning (at least trying) to love myself.

A clear moment of self-love–and pride–that stands out for me is when I was a sixth grader and was named captain of the school patrol. I had been on the patrol that year and to become captain felt like a grand achievement. I got to walk around the entire school grounds, in the morning and afternoons, to be sure all the other patrols were manning their assigned crosswalks and other stations, as kids came and went from school. I also had the one and only gold badge on my white shoulder belt. That was my first real glimpse of myself as a leader and what it was like to be entrusted with some real responsibility. I loved that feeling and I loved myself for having experienced that success. It certainly fueled a deeper desire to achieve and do well.

CHURCH RULES

A STRESSFUL MOMENT THAT was really a life-defining moment for me happened in church. We went to church every Sunday morning and night and then every Wednesday night for prayer services. No exceptions. Besides school, church was our life, it seemed. Never mind regular school homework, there were also lessons and Bible study we had to prepare for Sunday school.

I was nine years old when we were at a summer "revival" service. A revival meant we had to go to church every day at least once, sometimes twice. We were at a morning service and I kept hearing the preacher shouting, like he had been doing all that week, about how we would go to hell unless we were "saved." Between the shouting (which I am sure he would have described as being passionate) and imagining myself being in hell, I started feeling scared. That morning, the fear overwhelmed me and, in what seemed like a moment of panic, I jumped out of my seat to get down to the front of the church and be saved. The preacher put his hands on my head and told me to confess that I was a sinner and asked if I accepted Jesus as my lord and savior. Then the other women that were there gave me a hug and told me to pray with them. Then I was told I was saved. Those women seemed to love me.

I remember in the several days that followed, things seemed like a blur. My mom, especially, was crying a lot and saying how proud she was of me. I don't remember much from dad. The preacher and some other church people came to the house that Saturday and we prayed some more. They gave me a new Bible. I was confused over all the attention and why mom was crying so much. In the back of my mind, I knew the question of why this is such a big deal, was getting tucked away for a later time. For the moment, the fear had subsided and that felt good. I somehow knew Jesus and God loved me.

SUMMERS WITH GRANDAD LANE

As I got older, my parents would let me spend part of my summers with my grandparents. Those were certainly working vacations, as my maternal grandad Perry Lane never stopped working–except for naps after lunch! Well, there were also the times he would take me and my cousins to the river to swim and play on the sand bars. And yeah, the trips to town to get a snow cone were always a great break. I knew without a doubt grandad Lane loved me . . . and all 10 of his grandchildren.

But the thing most formative about those summers was getting to help my grandad by being his "farm hand".

Those deeper desires to excel were truly fostered during those times. Grandad taught me bundles about work ethic and personal integrity, while having fun and always staying curious. He drove home that sense of curiosity each time I would arrive for a visit, when he would start by taking me to the car barn (it was a garage as far as I was concerned) to see his collection of gadgets. On one wall of the car barn, he had nailed all sorts of mechanical type objects – old wrenches, gear assemblies, railroad tie spikes, parts from plows, small tools, big nuts and bolts and an array of other stuff he would find on the roadside or around other farms. The "arrival drill" was to find what he had added since the last visit. Then he would tell the story of how he found it and how he thought it was originally used. He would always ask me too to guess where I thought it came from or how it could have been used. After grandad died, my uncle took all of those objects off the wall of the car barn and made a display box for all ten cousins, with an assortment of those pieces for each of us. I still have it in my office, and it serves as a never-ending reminder of Perry's love that enveloped me in so many ways as a kid growing up.

On the farm, I got to ride along on the back of a plow on specially built seats (when I think of it now, I would never let my kids do something so dangerous) but, of course, the really big deal was graduating to be able to drive the tractor. At first in the seat with grandad and later as the sole driver. There were the times of hauling hay bales to the barn and stacking them in the loft. Pumping well water at the windmill into the water tank on the trailer, to go fill a trough out in the field for the cows. Tending the watermelon patch and getting to split open a ripe melon and eat just the heart of the melon. Grandad liked to leave the rest for the birds, he always said. He taught me to love mother nature, her bounty and the many creatures around us – including a healthy respect for rattlesnakes!

The summer that brought the best, lasting memory for the two of us as a team, was when I was twelve or maybe thirteen. That summer we built a new barbed-wire fence across a pasture at Fred's place. Fred was my grandfather's best friend and favorite dominoes partner. It felt like it was a mile-long fence, but in reality, it was probably a couple hundred yards or so. Grandad had me doing the hard, physical work, like digging the post holes, driving the metal corner posts far enough into the ground to be solid and sturdy, and stretching the wire tight enough for him to secure it to each post. I was also old enough to be tall enough to reach the gas and brake pedals of the old pick-up truck he used in the fields. So, of course, the best part was getting to drive the pick-up across the field, back to the "lay-down yard" near the house to load up more supplies.

Well actually, the very best part was that every summer after we built that fence, grandad would always drive the mile out of our way from town back to the farm, to show me the fence and declare with great pride "see . . . our fence is still standing!" Those moments were certainly filled with a great sense of pride for me too–for what we had done together and for what I had accomplished "on my own," away from mom and dad. As I look back at those times, I see the unconditional love that Grandad Lane brought into my life. He was such a strong role model in so many ways, yet the love I felt from him always was so clear and real. He made it easy for me to learn to love myself. His pride in my accomplishments gave me permission to experience my own sense of self-love. That was huge for me as a kid growing up.

RACISM, RELIGION AND CONDITIONAL LOVE

I'M SORRY TO SAY that the lingering memory I carry of my paternal grandfather was how vivid an example he was of what a racist is like. As that young boy growing-up during those summers in southern Oklahoma, I saw what racism looks like up-close. I remember standing there as a seven-year-old, aghast at how my grandfather could spew slurs and express so much hate about somebody else, especially someone that he didn't even know. I knew it was wrong and I am thankful that my parents did not bring that into our home. I will always be grateful that both my parents broke that cycle of hate and raised me and my three siblings with more awareness around race and our differences.

Yet I realize that racism is in my blood, given my paternal grandfather's view of the world . . . and while I believe that it does not define how I am in the world today, I know there have been and still may be ways that it has crept into my behavior, directly and indirectly. I know I can do everything I can to be aware and yet, I can still say and do things that expose my implicit racism. In that moment of first encountering someone different from me, do I turn away or turn toward them? Do I wonder about them or do I embrace the possibility of a chance to learn about someone new? Do I bless them in love or hurry past them in fear?

Racism, for me, is the epitome of conditional love, as well as implicit and explicit judgment of others and how it can play out in our lives (my life) every single day. My grandparents were seemingly comfortable with their racism and the conditional love that it brought into the world. My parents saw it differently, which enabled me to see the world in a more accepting way. Fast forward to today where, in my belief system, we are all interconnected, we are all a part of the same Source energy. What happens to one of us, impacts all of us.

Yes, differences were tolerated in our home... except when it came to religion. Religion was another lesson for me in the limits of conditional love. We were Southern Baptist and, my mom especially, was always very clear that our religion was the "right religion". What we believed is what everyone else should believe too . . . especially if they didn't want to go to hell. Yeah, that "go to hell" thing again. It was quite a pervasive theme throughout my growing up – or at least that seems to be what stood out. Never mind the "loving thy neighbor" part, which I do remember; it just did not seem to carry the same punch for me that the fear-laden message of "going to hell" did. (I was good however, because I had been saved.)

I now realize how the religious context at home and church caused an internal struggle around learning to truly love myself. If I was indeed a born sinner, how could I love myself if God was struggling to love me—or at least loving me conditionally until I could be saved? It was the source of what I later heard described as my "religious wounding". This is certainly not a condition unique to me by any stretch of the imagination. It is a big part of the set-up for living in a world defined by conditional love.

I remember clearly at age twelve, having a true epiphany around religion. It just hit me one day, that there was no way the rest of the people in the world could all be going to hell just because they didn't have the same religion and believe exactly the same thing that we did. There was just no way that made any sense to me at all. That realization was so clear for me in that moment. It was like a huge weight was lifted off of me and all of the sudden I felt lighter and freer than I could ever remember. It was a moment of true knowing . . . and it was also a moment I knew I had to keep to myself.

There was no way there could have been any type of conversation about this epiphany with my parents or even with most of my friends at that time. So, I held that knowing in silence for years, all the while continuing through the motions of all the church-related activities that were required. I suppose I could say I secretly loved myself for having broken-free of a big burden of fear that I had been carrying for years. In retrospect, that was the beginning of my spiritual journey and represented a clear shift in my own consciousness.

As I gained perspective years later, I saw the conditions my parents placed on their love for us kids. I always felt a clear love from mom and dad. I saw their love extend to my sisters, Susan and Barbara, and to my brother Tim. There were always family activities, especially around church-related events. It was a loving home environment and I always felt safe and encouraged to have fun, bring friends over and goof-off. But there were expectations on how to behave, what grades were acceptable at school, what was required regarding church and a myriad of other conditions essential to keeping things in good order with mom and dad. All normal type stuff, I suppose. It was just what was needed, I later realized, to maintain that loving atmosphere. I knew when I had disappointed either or both parents and that my job was to not let it happen again. I hardly ever remember getting yelled at much less being physically spanked. I just knew from the stern words from dad and the silent treatment from mom that I had screwed-up and left them disappointed. I learned it did not feel good to leave them disappointed. The psychological shadow of not ever feeling "good enough" found its way deep into my psyche. I had a really hard time loving myself, while trying to do what was needed to maintain an experience of my parents loving me.

ACCOMPLISHMENT AND THE JOY OF JOBS

I SUPPOSE THAT LEARNING to not disappoint my parents was what created the drive to achieve academically. While I wasn't always a straight-A student, I always made sure I came close. I also think avoidance of disappointment added to my work ethic and the flow of summer jobs once I got old enough to be employed. In all honesty, the bigger drivers for summer jobs really came from learning about work ethics, from watching my dad and learning from Grandad Lane. Dad was a petroleum engineer and mostly had a 9-to-5 job, but it was always clear to me how hard he worked and the pride he took in his work. He also taught me about integrity and being able to stand up for your beliefs.

I remember one time in particular when we were in a congregational meeting at church. It was some big-deal discussion on finances or something important like that. My father was a church deacon and I clearly recall seeing him stand-up at a pivotal moment in the meeting and make the declaration: "I concur with the chairman" (of the deacons) on a matter that went against what the pastor wanted. I knew he was taking a chance standing up for what he believed was right. My quiet sense of pride for my father, opened a window into loving myself as I created accomplishments of my own.

One of the times I felt my dad's overwhelming love and support came the summer I was fifteen years old. The church had started building a new sanctuary and somehow, he convinced his good friend the foreman to hire me as a laborer for a summer job. I was thrilled at the chance to have a "real job," especially one that had such prestige as being a construction worker. (McDonalds hadn't even opened their first store at that time!)

I got all the menial tasks, like sweeping up the building material debris left behind by the carpenters, pushing wheelbarrows of cement for the brick masons, and actually mixing up the mortar for them. The really big achievement came late that summer. I had apparently proven myself enough, that the foreman wanted to give me a job that carried much more responsibility and was more of a safety risk. He wanted me to start helping the masons on the scaffolding as they were working their way up the walls of the new building, setting the brick and the stones encasing the large stained glass windows at the sides and back of the building. I was to help keep them supplied with brick and mortar. I was fifteen and even then, back in 1966, I suppose I was legally under-aged for that type of work. I remember the foreman telling me about the job and that he had to talk to my dad first, to get his permission.

I was on pins and needles waiting for the decision and when my dad told me that evening that he was going to allow me to do the job, I was ecstatic. It was a big deal assignment for me but the really big deal was gaining my father's approval to do it. I felt his love, his pride, his joy in being able to tell me his decision. He amplified that pride as he told me how the foreman had spoken so highly about how I was handling the work. It was a moment of father-son bonding that still brings chills today. I came away from that summer with a new sense of my own character and a pride in achieving something really significant for me. I loved myself completely in that moment. I loved and felt a deep respect for my dad too, for how he encouraged me to take the job in the first place and then how he supported me to make it something I never would have suspected possible.

I see now how that summer boosted my sense of self and my self-confidence. It set me up for a really strong finish for my remaining high school years. I experienced what "finding my voice" felt like in speech class and even developed my own identity with humor. (Please don't ask me to do the Smothers Brothers routine on "Mom Always Liked You Best," that became my signature breakout moment!). I went on through high school to gain National Honor Society academic recognition, reveled in being named a boy-of-the-month my senior year and subsequent leadership (or maybe popularity) awards. I think I really did love myself, as much as it seemed everyone else loved me. My awareness of self had grown big-time through high school and while I didn't use the term at that point, I had also seen my consciousness expand as I gained a better sense of who

I was. At some level I was gaining a deeper ability to love myself just for who I was.

COMING OF AGE AND A DEVASTATING LOSS

I HAD FUN BEING a teenager in the 60s. I had my first romantic love in high school. We dated my sophomore and junior years and then her family moved out of state. I tried dating a few other girls my senior year, but none captured my attention in the same way. I'll continue that part of the story later . . . in Lifetime #2.

Getting my first car, a 1947 Oldsmobile sedan, gaining more independence, and having a few older friends enabled some acting out that really stressed things on the home front. Without dwelling on the details (especially about starting to experiment with drinking and smoking), I will just say it pressed my relationship with mom and dad. One way it came to a head was around decision time on what college to attend. I had my heart first set on an out-of-state school (Rice University in Houston) that dad had to tell me they could not afford. My next choice (Oklahoma University) turned out to be the rival state university to my dad's alma mater (Oklahoma State University), and OU also had the reputation of being a big party school. There was no way he was going to pay for me going there–he really dug-in and became totally insistent that I attend the same university he did and that I study engineering, like he did. I was good in math and science and was leaning towards engineering anyway, but it became a bittersweet decision because of our conflict over making it all happen his way. It left me feeling bitter and beat-down.

I left home for college with what could be called some "bad blood" between me and my parents, especially my dad. I was really glad to get out of the house and be free of the constant oversight. There was certainly a feeling of a very shaky love as I drove away. Deep down I resented the hell out of how it all went down. That was pretty much the defining set-up for my freshman year. The Beatles had a song out several years earlier, called "Nowhere Man" and it spoke quite loudly to my state of mind.

There were certainly some good moments and events as a freshman, but I was still in a state of feeling lost for a number of reasons. Those are not so important for now, as that was all to change with the phone call I got from home, the day after my last freshman final exam. Mom was instructing me to come home that day, because dad was going into the hospital for open-heart surgery the next morning. Open. Heart. What??!!??

It was the first time I had heard about how serious things had gotten for dad that year, while I was away.

He had the first of his three heart attacks at the age of 33 (I was 10 at that time) so I was well aware of his heart condition, but it was a total shock to hear he was having major surgery. I remember getting so angry at mom for not telling me what was going on sooner. It turned out they had both made the decision to "not upset me" with the news before finals.

I got to the hospital in time to see dad, just before they took him into the OR. He looked pale and weak, yet he managed a smile and a "hello son, I'll see you in a bit" before the doors closed behind him. That was the last time I saw him alive.

Open-heart (quadruple) bypass surgery had just started to be a thing in the late 60s and was still a relatively new procedure in 1970. He made it through the surgery, but some (I don't remember what) complication set in and he died in the recovery room. My mom got to go in moments before he passed, but I was not allowed to be in with them. His mom, my paternal grandmother, was with me in the waiting room when we got the news. My two sisters and brother were at home with our aunt and uncle.

It was a long drive home, to say the least. My sisters, Sue and Barb, remember more about what happened next than I do. I just remember that breaking the news to them and my little brother Tim was the most painful experience I had ever had up to that point in my life.

Needless to say, our lives were all changed forever. What ensued that summer, as we struggled to deal with the grief and loss, was a complete mess. Mom was never able to say much to any of us about her inability to handle her grief. However, she wrote in a short memoir before she died that she knew she was completely lost and did not know how to help any of us through that period of loss, much less herself.

My first life had abruptly ended.

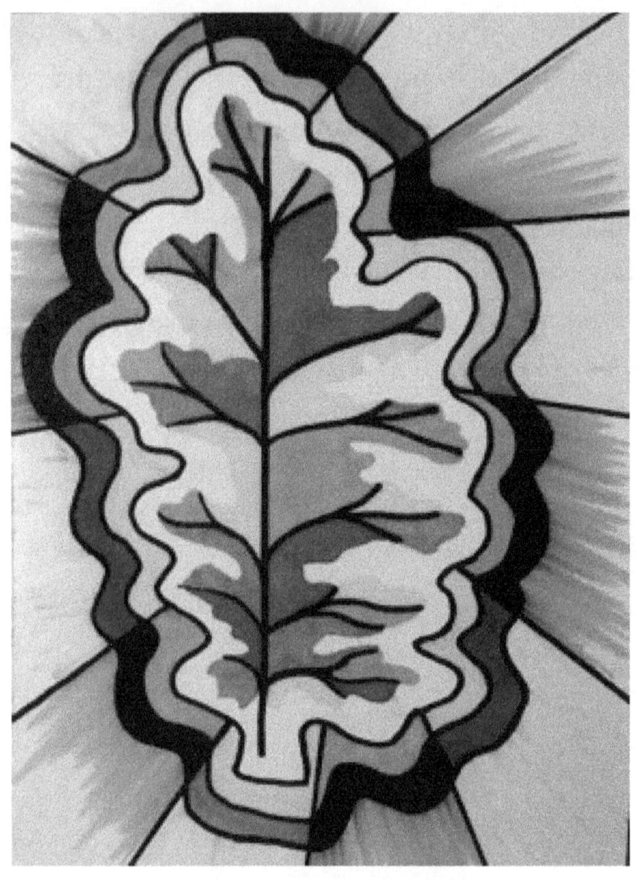

Original artwork by Rosemary Renee' Davis - ©2021

Lifetime #1
Perspectives

MY EXPERIENCE OF LOVE

I KNOW HOW MUCH my parents loved me . . . it was always a loving home environment. I know I always felt love for my parents. Even through the teenage years of my own rebellion, there was a deep love for mom and dad.

I know the love my grandparents had for me and especially how that felt with Grandad Lane.

With my siblings, extended family, church family and so many friends, I knew what love felt like both given and received.

This loving environment at home also held the big contrast of what I came to understand as conditional love—the love that was dependent on my behavior, attitudes and accomplishments. I now know of course that conditional love was not unique to my experience.

Both my experiences of being well-loved on the one hand and being loved conditionally on the other influenced the development (or lack) of my self-love. My self-love was evident when I think about my care-free and playful life as a kid growing up. I loved myself fully in all of those moments of freedom and joy. I reveled in the attention of my grandparents and it was easy in those times to love myself for all I was and was becoming.

As I grew older, I struggled in the face of growing expectations, especially around school and religion, and that struggle created deep doubts about my own sense of self-worth. By the time I reached high school and had stepped into a clear phase of rebellion, I experienced a lot of internal conflict in trying to find my own self. The self that was being defined by parental expectations was clear to me each day, however I was lost to the idea of any true awareness of self-love of the "real" me. It led me to embrace that idea of being a "Nowhere Man."

MY EVOLUTION IN CONSCIOUSNESS

I NOW BELIEVE THE "Nowhere Man" condition emerged from the (unknown at the time) impact of the 'conditional love' environment at home. Of course, it was all a subconscious thing going on. I am no psychologist; however, I now am aware of a number of those self-worth messages I took on and buried in my psyche. They included: my voice didn't matter, my feelings weren't important, my anger was not acceptable and that I couldn't be loved for just who I was. I know this now from having done a lot of work on expanding my self-awareness and consciousness in my adult years.

Perhaps the single largest jump in my consciousness growing up was my "knowing" at age twelve that our religion was not absolute, although I didn't know to describe it like that back then.

I see now that this conscious knowing was fueled by my grappling with the fear of going to hell for my "sinning" and the anguish of going through the process of being "saved" at that church revival. It led to the stirring of and then deep discomfort around my religion being so restrictive and absolute. The knowing was also fueled by a deep-down sense of compassion for everyone else in the world, especially those that weren't Southern Baptist! I believe it was finally anchored in my growing awareness that God really was loving of everyone, rather than judgmental and damning.

Another facet of my emerging consciousness was an awareness that the seeds of seeing the world through the lens of unconditional love, were planted in how my parents broke the explicit cycle of racism that they had grown-up with in their homes. Their tolerance at least helped me see the way toward some level of acceptance and at the time, that created a small (and yet unknown) shift in my consciousness.

However, I was still a very long way from realizing that it might be possible to live every day in the consciousness that is experienced as unconditional love.

A MOMENT TO REFLECT . . . ON LIFETIME #1

As I recall the joy of my childhood, I have a sense of warm, calm joy inside. I can savor the delight and fun that was present so often. I smile as I think about how simple it all was, yet how it was so carefree and so clearly defined by the love of my family.

I see the progression clearly now, the unconditional love through childhood, turning into conditional love driven by the best of desires and expectations, as I grew older. Then at some (teenage) point, I experienced shifting into resentment and rebellion, culminating in a devastating loss, which surfaced guilt about how I left things with dad. While I see where the trajectory of all of this left me as my first life ended, I also know the ever-growing sense of myself that came with that progression.

I can clearly see the evolving love of self that was happening even if, at the time, it was not quite so evident. I can feel the pride of accomplishment, the pride of self and the awareness of more of who I was and who I am.

That awareness is what strikes me now as the undercurrent that has propelled me forward to today. I have moved through so many negative and positive feelings about myself. All of it has been conspiring to open my mind and my heart to who I am today. That awareness that I am a spiritual being having a human experience. That understanding that I am here to have an opportunity to continue to grow on a spiritual level and with that growth to continually expand my own level of consciousness. And with that expansion comes a sense of the huge gift living this life is all about for me. I accept this gift; I nurture this gift and I express the depth of my gratitude for this gift.

Original heartwork by Jaxon Wesley Davis - ©2021

Lifetime #2 - The Pathway of Idyllic Love

LIFETIME #2 STARTED IN the aftermath of dad's death, however, it was two years later that my focus dramatically shifted, when that young love that started in high school turned into marriage as I was finishing college. Those early years of marriage were fun-filled and seemingly carefree as we nurtured the love that brought us together. Then there was the joy of two children filling our lives, coming within fifteen months of each other.

My 2nd Life adventure went into high gear when we moved overseas and spent four years living in Malaysia, traveling to many amazing places throughout the world. It was then that a focus on career began to dominate and our loving partnership turned into a blur. As the turbulence of an accelerating career set in our once idyllic love shattered. Then came divorce and the grief of a loss that "wasn't supposed to happen".

In the aftermath of divorce, a sudden turn happened for me that allowed me to find my way back to myself.

There was a surprising recovery of self-love and an explosion of personal and spiritual growth began.

• CHAPTER 2 •

Work, Marriage, Kids ... and Divorce

THE SUMMER AFTER DAD died, I was given a job by his oil company Texaco as a roustabout in the oilfields near our home in Tulsa. I was able to live at home and help (sort of) navigate through the intense fallout and grief from dad dying. Mom was lost. We all were lost. We had prayer "vigils" each night on the living room couch, in an effort to console ourselves and ultimately help mom find a way to cope and hold it together for her four kids.

She had always been a stay-at-home mom, never worked after she and dad were married. Fortunately, we had some insurance money that helped us through until she was able to go back to school and then get a job. Looking back on that summer, we were trying to simply survive, while figuring out how to carry on with our lives, individually and as a family. The love within our family seemed lost in the grief and confusion. We would hug and hold each other, cry together and watch, as mom would fall apart and then retreat to her bedroom to try to collect herself yet again.

For me, the oilfield work that summer was my real escape. I really don't remember that I did any of the traditional grieving. I'm sure I cried some at the funeral and perhaps occasionally at our evening prayer vigils. I just don't remember feeling the purge of letting the grief flow through me. I do remember the welcome relief of working with those other men in the oil fields. It was hard physical work, made harder by a foreman who was out to test the stamina of a young college kid. By the end of the summer, he and I were getting along in a good way. My sense of achievement kicked in as a result!

I went back to college in the fall and started working essentially full time to pay for my education while taking my engineering classes. It felt like I essentially abandoned my siblings, and in all honesty, it was a relief to be back in school. It would be years before we would even touch on what that was like for each of us during that time immediately after losing dad.

FIRST COMES LOVE, THEN COMES MARRIAGE, THEN COMES...

THE ROMANCE THAT HAD started for me in high school, picked up again in college. After dad died, I had done what I could on my own to refocus myself on school and on my new need to support myself. Suzie was in school at Baylor, and we went from corresponding and phone calls to weekend visits when class schedules allowed. We married the summer before my senior year.

Suzie put her education on hold and went to work, so I could finish my degree and then go on to graduate school to get my master's in engineering. School was demanding, her work was nonstop, and yet we were madly in love and having a great time starting a life together. It was deep, romantic love of fun proportions and it gave us a chance to grow together as a couple.

After graduation, we moved out of state to St. Louis for my new job and she restarted her college work. Those five years or so before kids came along were fun, carefree and filled with friends, camping, concerts, skiing and family visits at the holidays. It felt idyllic. We were together, committed, growing through shared experiences, and simply enjoying our life as a married couple.

Then the blessing of our two children came along. Our son Adam was born in the middle of a winter storm that dumped 24" of snow on the streets and fifteen months later, on a beautiful spring morning, our daughter Emily entered the world. Talk about the experience of love expanding. It happened big time with our son and daughter and they became the focus of our lives. Becoming a father was a clear experience for me of giving out the most unconditional love I could imagine. I know the kids gave it right back to me, especially as we played hard together during our games of "tickle-tackle."

Suzie had stopped working to focus on raising the kids and I began the drive to build my career and work harder for our financial well-being. I had been promoted to a project engineer and was part of a team building new electronic industry plants in the US and Asia. My job required that I start traveling, first on domestic assignments, which would take me away a week at a time for what turned out to be months on end. That started taking its toll in a number of ways. Suzie essentially became a single mom raising the kids during the week and I would sweep-in on weekends to (sort of) provide some relief. It was somewhere during that time that I also started a weekend MBA program, because I became convinced it was a faster path to bigger and better jobs in my budding corporate career.

Looking back, that budding career created a faster path to a troubled marriage. My work-life balance suffered with a heavier workload each time I got promoted and continued work travel. I came home one weekend to discover Suzie had really had it with me being away so much. We had a huge falling-out and I thought I was going to lose everything. I was so upset I don't even remember if the kids were around that weekend—but they were only six and seven, so of course they were there. It felt like my world was imploding. I was enraged and scared, looking for what I needed to do to hold my family together.

A NEW LIFE OVERSEAS

WHAT HAPPENED NEXT WOULD shape our lives for years to come in many unexpected ways. As we were dealing with the consequences of the huge marital rift that had been created, I was offered a big job overseas. It was one of those career moves that could not be turned down. We somehow sucked it up on the personal side, got past the bitterness (actually, we just buried it deep enough to be out of sight) and moved to Malaysia. The kids were starting first and second grades, I was starting a significant new assignment and Suzie was starting a period of being so lost and feeling so out of place, that a deep despair set in. For a while I thought we were going to have to move back to the States.

I actually have no idea where the love we had for so long had gone. I know I was on automatic pilot and I think she was as well. We eventually made some friends, found the expat party circuit, began traveling around the region and settled in, more or less, to a new life in a new country with endless new experiences.

The kids will tell you about how that overseas life experience has shaped their world view. They discovered the richness that cultural diversity can bring as they were in school with kids from every imaginable part of the world. They discovered a whole new culinary world at the food stalls and beachside villages we visited. They also discovered they loved flying in first class—it was much better than, what they aptly began to call, "last class."

I will tell you (and I think Suzie would too) that things buried, somehow find a way of resurfacing if unaddressed. The hurt and devastation of our fall-out began to bring out an anger in both of us that was fierce at times. It usually happened after we had been partying with friends, when we would come back home and find ourselves in alcohol-induced arguments. The yelling and screaming was intense and so unexpected. I have no idea what awareness the kids have of those times. They never seemed to wake up during the arguments.

At least we held it together during the daytime as we continued our lives and the great adventure we were having in foreign lands. But the pain and drain of the arguments eventually caught up with us, and as we were nearing the end of our time as expats, things went from bad to worse. It was all an accumulation from the hurt that was never really mended. Our divide was so intense at that point that it shattered what little love was left between us.

We stumbled through several years after moving back home and finally decided to divorce, though I resisted it all along the way. I had this notion in my mind that we had to gut it out and try to find a way to stay together. Looking back, I was so emotionally unavailable that I couldn't have been a good partner to anyone. Finally, I agreed to call it quits. When we told the kids about the decision to divorce, our son Adam bolted and became a road kid, dropping out of high school. Our daughter Emily managed to get herself through her last years of high school, pretty much on her own.

They say time heals old wounds and, in our case, I believe it to be true. Today, some thirty years later, when Suzie and I text or talk, it will often include an expression of love, in one way or another. It is always heart-felt. The love we had for each other has seemed to find its way back into our lives in a quiet, open way. We both did a lot of our own inner work to get to this point.

MY INWARD JOURNEY BEGINS

My intentional personal and spiritual growth work actually started as we were in the final stage of our married life together. I went into therapy as a way to try to cope with the divorce that was imminent. This was actually the beginning of the path back to a sense of self-love that had been buried in the turmoil of breaking up . . . and before, if I were to be really honest.

I remembered at one point in therapy–and several times later–declaring that "it wasn't supposed to be this way". We were supposed to stay together through thick and thin, at least in the belief system I had been hanging on to for a long time.

In therapy, I also discovered a really big pattern that I had been unconsciously playing out through those twenty-three years of marriage. In a way, I had been ignoring what felt important to me and deferring to Suzie's wishes to be sure she was always happy. I had been stuffing down my feelings about things, just so the appearance of peace could be kept. Sort of. This was never a conscious awareness I had at the time. It was only through therapy that I came to understand what has turned out to be a really big lesson to learn for myself. I see now that it was a reflection of how little self-love I had been holding. That understanding alone was a huge awakening of consciousness.

I then had an experience that was as much physical as it was emotional. It felt as if my heart had been broken apart leaving me open and vulnerable. It just came spontaneously for no apparent reason. It was a Sunday morning when it happened, and I spent most of the day in tears. I remember going alone to the church we attended and slipping into the back pew where no one else was sitting. It was a comforting place and through the entire service, I sat sobbing, just letting the tears flow. I left quietly just before the service ended, so I would not have to explain myself at that moment to any of my friends there. This whole experience left me able to know and express my feelings, which I had never felt able to do before. A self-love was beginning to re-emerge.

I began to develop some clarity around the difference between religion and spirituality and decided to take a huge step into seeking my spiritual growth. This was facilitated by my minister at the time. It was a very bonding experience for us and he essentially became a spiritual counselor for me. In meditations, I opened to the presence of my spiritual guides. There was the little girl (who threw a book at me) and was encouraging me to find more playfulness in my life; there was a golden orb, which I will discuss in detail shortly, that was bringing me wisdom and knowledge; and there were two men in the woods who appeared to support me and be with me during the difficulties of my divorce.

Part of my spiritual journey was also connecting on a deeper level with Barbara, my "kid sister". We were living in different cities and over the phone we discussed all these new experiences and tried to sort out all that was changing in my life at the time. She became an anchor, an ally and confidant at a time I truly needed it.

One other big shift for me in the months before my marriage ended, was my decision to completely break with drinking. I needed to gain clarity around the growth in self-love that was happening without the interference of alcohol.

All of these were steps toward my reclaiming of myself. I was shedding many old beliefs and exploring new ideas, reading personal growth and spiritual books nonstop, and an entirely new world was opening up for me. It wasn't quite unconditional love for myself yet, but it was close.

There was a rather significant and fortuitous expression of feelings that happened before Suzie and I separated. We made the choice to engage in what essentially became a reconciliation process. For three to four nights in a row, we sat down to go back through our twenty-three years together. Knowing the marriage was ending, we made it a time to say what we needed to say—everything that we had not said in the last 2+ decades.

We talked through all the rough spots and all the hurt and damage we had brought into each other's lives in a truly loving way. We made it a time of creating closure and healing. And yes, more self-love became evident, as did the love we had shared together for each other.

There were two other defining moments for me in the second lifetime, both of which also occurred before we actually separated. One happened just as we had made the decision on when to separate, sell the house, and go our separate ways while the official divorce proceedings played out with the lawyers.

One of our last Saturdays together, I got up and was doing chores around the house. Out of nowhere, I began to feel this warmth envelope me, like a soft vibrational blanket surrounding me. It was the most peaceful, serene feeling I had ever experienced. I found Suzie and asked if she was noticing anything like it and she said no. I explained what I was experiencing and was able to describe it as feeling like I was being held in a perfect, all-encompassing love. I sat for a while and it just stayed with me. I had to start doing some other things and it stayed with me. Throughout the whole day, that night and most of the next day I was held in this unbelievable feeling of love. Love that was bigger than I had ever known, love that was clear, unconditional and totally there for me and, as I tried to explain to Suzie, I thought it was being offered for us, as well. I was in a state of bliss yet kept functioning as close to normal as I could. I knew all was going to be okay in my life going forward. I knew it was all okay just as it was at that point in time.

This experience of unconditional love surrounding me, the many new steps of personal growth I was experiencing, our reconciliation process, the discovery of my spiritual side were all part of what I now believe set me up for that second definitive moment . . . and what then became a series of experiences.

MY OUT OF BODY JOURNEYS BEGIN

One Saturday morning, out of the blue, I had a spontaneous out of body experience (OBE). I felt myself separate from my physical body and float upwards. I found myself looking down on my physical body lying there on the couch. I started seeing shapes, objects, symbols clearly above me and all around me. Then a huge yellow-gold object that was spinning very fast came very close past my right ear. As it passed by, I very clearly heard the sound of it spinning, it was a strange hum and buzz. It was rounded in nature but looked like a cut prism ball, like the crystal ones in a jewelry collection or like a disco ball. It went to the end of the room where it hovered briefly then came back and stopped right in front of me. I could hear the humming again very clearly. It was quite loud. I hovered there and just took it in. It was a brilliant color with a yellow-gold glow around it. After a few moments it shot out of the bedroom through the window.

Then I felt myself following it across the room. I could feel no force on me, I was weightless. I went toward the window and I remember bracing myself as I passed through the wall and out into the air outside the house—but I didn't actually feel anything. I could hear myself saying "I am with you, I am with you" and as I looked down I was hovering over the swimming pool in the backyard. Then the experience ended, and I was back in my body lying on the couch.

I remember the sensation of feeling alert and in a strange state of awareness. Then I began to hear the piano music that had been playing all along on the CD player. My mind was very clear having come back into my body and I immediately recorded what I experienced in my journal.

Over the next two years, I went on to have dozens of OBEs. I learned from a spiritual teacher and medium that the Golden Orb I experienced was one of my spirit guides, there to bring me wisdom and knowledge around all I was encountering in my life.

There were many lessons in each of these OBEs for me to learn:

Love myself.
Be in the moment.
Express my feelings.
Face my fears.
Seek out knowledge and wisdom and continue to understand my spiritual journey.
Learn to be childlike and have more fun.

I was also encouraged by the spiritual teacher who told me that I have much to share and can help many people, that I should share everything I experience, and it is important that I do. Perhaps in my next life I was to be a preacher or lecturer or a speaker on hope.

Maybe the most significant learning that came from all of those experiences was an understanding that we are more than our physical bodies and that the essence of who we are–our Souls, our Higher Selves, our Consciousness - continues on after we die our physical deaths.

This big life-changing understanding is such a significant part of my story; it has allowed me to experience the "Universal Love" that surrounds us all and that is the fundamental make-up of all that we are. I didn't try to make this happen, it just did, and I can now see and say what a huge gift it has brought into my life. I will come back to this, with some additional insights, when I talk about my 4th Life.

These big experiences of my heart breaking open to my feelings, the Saturday surrounded in unconditional love and my OBEs all started me down the path of personal growth, emotional awareness, and spiritual seeking. As part of my spiritual journey, I began to realize how much the way we relate to each other needs to change. That the on-going strife that feels so central to the human condition could be eliminated if we shifted to a higher level of consciousness, both on an individual and on the collective level. That it would only be from a higher level of consciousness that the unnecessary divisions and walls we put up to separate ourselves could be broken down.

From that higher consciousness, we will be able to see how we are all connected on a spiritual level and that we are all in this together. Knowing that connection and realizing we are all the same at the soul level will lead us to treat each other in a completely different way. We can treat each other with compassion, with unconditional love, and when we do, we will all start having a completely different experience, both in our individual lives and in our community life.

As you can see, it was a very explosive growth period for me and there was no turning back.

...

NOW IF YOU REMEMBER, I was telling the part of my story I now call my 2nd Life, and how it was actually coming to an end. The separation within the marriage happened, as the divorce proceedings were being finalized. The combination of my personal growth work and those related spiritual experiences helped propel me forward, even as my life was completely over as I knew it. And the thought kept lingering with me that, "it just wasn't supposed to be this way".

My 2nd Life literally ended when I moved into an apartment by myself (and with room for the kids). I had no idea what was going to happen next. No idea whatsoever.

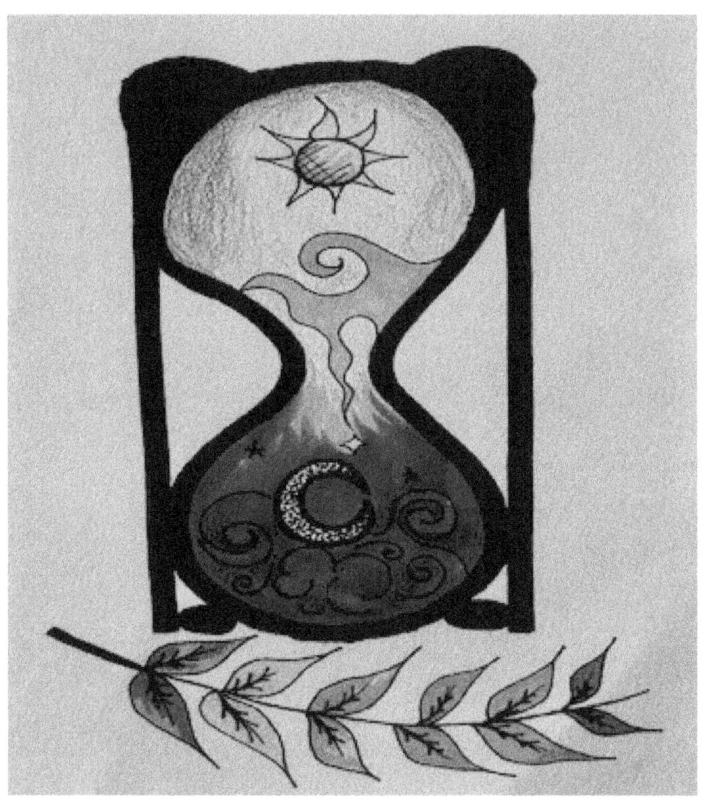

Original artwork by Rosemary Renee' Davis - ©2021

Lifetime #2 Perspectives

MY EXPERIENCE OF LOVE

LIFETIME #2 HELD SUCH a very rich experience of the depth of love (and fun times) within that first marriage. Yes, the marriage ended, and the conscious "reconciliation process" we created at the end resulted in at least partially finding our way back to the love that defined us from the start - at least that is how I would characterize it. It certainly brought a somewhat loving closure to a difficult time.

There was the really clear unconditional love experienced for and from our children, especially in their most formative years. Yes, the separation and then divorce strained that love as well, and we were to find our ways back to each other in the years ahead.

My big shift into an entirely new level of self-love happened with my heart literally opening-up to being able to experience all my feelings. I was surprised to find how blocked from my feelings I had been during those twenty+ years, yet I know now that things changed dramatically once I was ready to experience myself in that way. Yes, it was a big pathway that opened in my life journey, and it is still helping define my self-love today.

The love of supportive, caring and compassionate friends and family played a huge role in helping me navigate the challenges along the way in my 2nd Life, especially as the marriage was ending. I feel certain I never fully expressed my gratitude for the work with my spiritual counselor and yet I did feel a deep bond with him. There was (and is) a real depth of connection with my immediate family, especially at that time with both my mom and my younger sister. Yes, mom was there with a listening ear, and it was my sister that brought understanding and guidance at critical moments.

And yes, getting "in touch with my feelings" was the big shift in self-love, as was consciously choosing to make a break with drinking near the end of Lifetime #2. That was indeed another big act of self-love at that time in my life.

MY EVOLUTION IN CONSCIOUSNESS

LIFETIME #2 BROUGHT ME to a critical turning point in my consciousness journey when I took my huge step into seeking personal and spiritual growth. Something was ignited within and continues to fuel my desire to keep learning even today. It seems simple now, however the clarity I gained around the separation between religion and spirituality for me was so important. To realize I am at my essence a spiritual being connected directly to Source Energy or God or the Universe was a much-needed step in my evolution.

Discovering the presence of and experiencing my spiritual guides, including the little girl, the golden orb, and the two men in the woods opened a doorway into guidance I had never realized possible. I am so grateful for their on-going presence in my life and the quiet guidance I know that is always there. They are who I have come to call "My Dear Ones."

Learning through my out-of-body experiences that we are more than our physical bodies and that the essence of who we are continues after we die our physical deaths has been life changing. As those experiences continued, I was able to release a fear of death that continues to comfort me in such a loving way.

As I was watching my own movement and understanding of consciousness evolve in those "early days", that is when the question of our collective movement emerged. I came to a clarity around the shift I believe is needed–actually required–in our collective consciousness to a place of unconditional love. It was more of an intellectual understanding that surfaced then, yet it was the beginning of a much bigger exploration for me.

It was in that early exploration of my own consciousness that the seeds were being sown of seeing it might be possible to live every day in the level of consciousness that is experienced as unconditional love.

A MOMENT TO REFLECT . . . ON LIFETIME #2

THERE ARE SO MANY ways I could tell the story of my 2nd Life. What I have chosen is to illustrate the experiences that stand-out as I think about my own personal growth. Especially through the lens of unconditional love. When I step back and look at the overall progression I have written about, I see how I advanced in so many ways. That progression was book-ended by the loss of my father and then the loss of my marriage. I can see how life unfolded such that I was in the right place, at the right time, to experience such a leap in my spiritual growth and as a result, experience a significant jump in my own consciousness.

To have come to the end of the marriage and start to open in all the ways that I did and expand my sense of knowing, is quite another gift in how the Universe can orchestrate things. I feel so blessed and so fortunate to be able to have experienced it in this way and to see it with some clarity at this point in time. I am again so grateful to find this perspective.

I also feel a deep sense of compassion for the experience of my ex-wife and my two children, as they were really the focal point for me, throughout this Lifetime #2. I honor their experiences through this time and acknowledge the heartache and heartbreak I know I contributed to with them. At the same time, I hold them each in such a depth of love, appreciation and gratitude that my heart is full. My eyes overflow with tears when I think of what they (all 3) mean to me.

Lifetime #2 was a big life for me, in so many ways. I feel humbled even trying to articulate part of what that has meant. I feel so fortunate for all that it brought me and how I was able to learn and grow as a result. And that touches the love that is there at my very Essence.

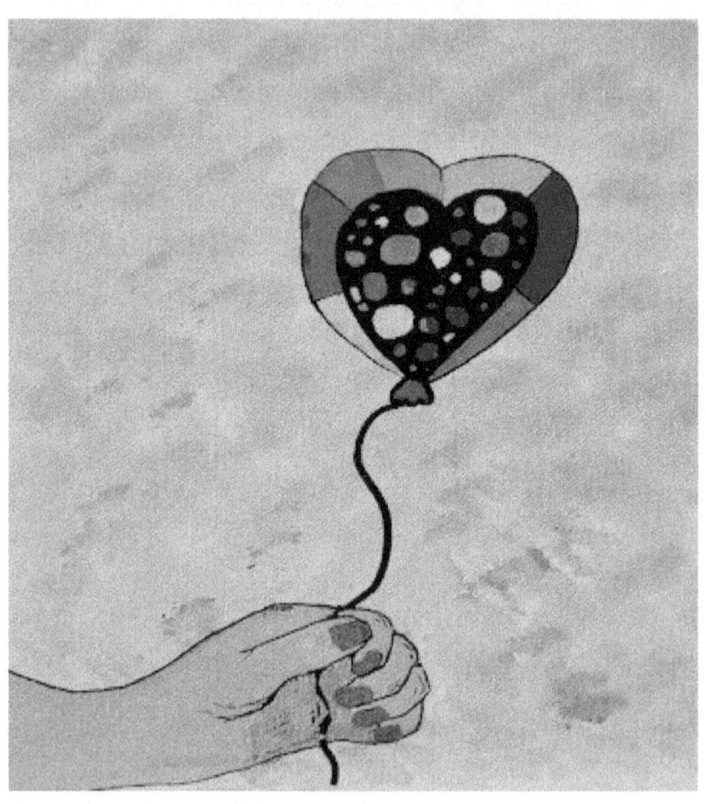

Original heartwork by Jaxon Wesley Davis - ©2021

Lifetime #3 - The Journey into Unconditional Love

It was out of that 2nd Life personal growth work that Lifetime #3 was born. I had found myself again and was feeling really clear about starting my new phase. "Finding myself" had indeed taken a lot of work and was still a work in progress. And while it was hard, it had brought me to a place of feeling invigorated, clear and excited about moving on.

It was 1994 and I was forty-three years old at that time. I had my moments of fear thinking about the future and an occasional bout with my anger around all that had happened in the past. However, it was a time of readiness to carry on with finding a new life.

One morning, about two months after I had settled into my new life-arrangement as a single, I was sitting at my office desk and I looked up . . . and there she was, this stunning blonde, standing there with this amazing smile and these very captivating blue eyes. While it was easy to see how I could have gotten distracted, she was there as the highly recommended positive psychologist who specialized in leadership consulting. We were about to discuss a work proposal she had submitted for the change management project I was in charge of implementing for the company. She was certainly cute, but we had business to discuss and anyway, I had been very clear with myself that I wanted nothing to do with another relationship for a long while. Turned out she was married anyway.

It also turned out she was the right person for the job, so I hired Kathy and her team to help us with the work project. That was the beginning of a big new phase for me, business-wise and personally as well.

Kathryn D. Cramer, PhD, was this dynamic, high energy, always so very positive person. She was confident, clear and quite creative. There was always a solution to any bump in the road and more often than not, she was seeing those bumps before we got to them and navigating the tough spots with ease. She got up to speed really quickly with the project and company dynamics and we were on a really good trajectory with the work.

That was the time I took a new job assignment; one I had been moving toward for some time. So, after about a month working to get Kathy and her team on board, I left to start our company's first joint venture in mainland China. Having lived in Malaysia and traveled extensively throughout Asia in my previous roles, I had some idea of what was in store.

I chose to not make a permanent move to China, so I could still have a chance at spending time with my children, given we were all trying to figure out our new lives since the separation. Just before my first trip to China in the new job, I checked in with Kathy on some of the details of the project she was handling. At the end of that meeting, she invited me to attend a book signing party she was having that next night. I knew she was an author as well as a consultant, but it had not come up that a new book was about to be released. It was her second book called *"Roads Home–Seven Pathways to Midlife Wisdom"*. The book was about the inner growth that is possible in midlife that was impossible earlier in life. It was part science, part psychology and part spiritual odyssey. My kind of reading at that time!

The signing party was at my favorite bookstore, so I dropped by to congratulate her and buy a copy of the book. I remember meeting her father and husband, amongst a sea of other family and friends. I didn't really know anyone, so made my way home early to get packed for my trip. As I was tucking the new book into my backpack, I read the words she had written when she signed my copy of her book: "To John - my newest best friend and colleague - this book was born out of a desire to keep growing so I can keep up with people like you!" I'll admit that brought a warm smile to my heart.

On the thirteen-hour flight to Beijing, I had time to read most of Kathy's new book. I began writing down questions and found myself mesmerized at how congruent so many of her thoughts were with my own beliefs and understandings. There I was in this tremendous time of personal growth and her book was offering so many ways to extend that growth. I was indeed captivated by her discussion on spiritual growth and how midlife often brings us deeper understanding of our consciousness, which closely paralleled so many of the same realizations I was having for myself.

When I returned three weeks later, I ran into her back at the office one day and started talking about my reaction to her book. I asked if we could find a time to go over some of my questions and comments and she agreed to meet me for a drink that Friday evening. We had a lot to talk about, once I started into my questions and we let the conversation go from there. It turned out, she too was actually separated from her husband and they had been living apart for several months. His presence at the book signing was a "keeping up appearances" kind of thing, she said.

Running into her that following week again at the office, I guess in a moment of feeling somewhat emboldened, I asked her if we could continue our conversation and also discuss the work project over dinner that weekend. She agreed. She was living about an hour outside of town and so we decided to meet at a restaurant at a halfway point.

That dinner meeting turned out to be a night that would come back to both haunt me - and thrill me - for the next twenty+ years. It was about halfway through the dinner, when Kathy stopped eating and asked . . . "is this a business meeting or a date?" My answer to that question is what came back to haunt me. I replied, "I'm not sure!" Kathy never let me forget that moment. However, it turned out to be a good enough answer because when we finished dessert, she asked me if I wanted to come back to her Innsbrook lake house for a "night cap."

While I barely remember the drive back to my apartment that next day, deep down I knew that would be the last time I would say to Kathy, "I'm not sure." It was a great lesson on listening to my heart, trusting my gut or any other way of describing when a "knowing" is waiting in the background to emerge and overshadow a doubt.

As I look back, that night at Innsbrook was the real start of my 3rd Life. We started dating and seeing each other every time I was home—I was spending about half my time away, working in China. It was around three months into the relationship, when I heard myself admit, out loud (to myself), that I was indeed falling in love and to just let that be okay and see what happens. Three years later, we were married.

From the start, this was the kind of a relationship that I could never have imagined. Kathy and I had an amazing connection from the beginning, in every way possible. The experience of falling in love, being in love with Kathy and creating a life together was beyond my wildest dreams. We were together almost twenty-two years, married a month short of nineteen years, when she died. But let me linger for a while on those twenty-two years because they were the years that brought me –and us–this incredible journey into a lived experience of unconditional love.

Falling in love with Kathy during the three years before we were married brought the early realization that unconditional love was actually something real . . . and all of the sudden it was real in my life! My life! Not in a movie or a story, an actual lived experience in which I found myself! I was able to open in new ways to self-love because of experiencing Kathy loving me so unconditionally. Her love allowed me to understand myself in a way that had not been possible before. It felt like a miracle to be loved so unconditionally by another, by Kathy.

And what an even greater miracle to begin realizing I could love myself in that same way. How could I have gone all that time not even realizing how much I had been holding back from accepting myself as I truly was? This experience unfolded, expanded, and grew beyond belief over those next twenty years.

After ten years together, Kathy and I merged our careers. By that time in my corporate career, I had moved into strategic planning and a lot more change management work. With that came the beginning of my executive coaching, my team development, and large meeting facilitation work. This was all very similar in many ways to what Kathy was doing. When I was within a year of making the decision to retire, Kathy and I started talking about my coming to work with her at The Cramer Institute (TCI). When the time came to say goodbye to the corporate world, we had a good plan in place on how I could fit in and expand the work in the consulting world.

Before starting the actual day-to-day working of that plan, I took off three or four months just to clear my head and heart from the remnants of my corporate life. I used that time to build an outdoor kitchen and bar at our new pool and to develop my focus for entering the consulting world at The Cramer Institute. That is when I gained my initial clarity around my desire to help others gain more self-awareness and their own clarity about what they are bringing into the world.

At first my work with Kathy consisted of a learning process with her helping me gain a deep understanding of the clients and the work in progress. For that first year or so, Kathy and I saw each other almost every day just like any other coworker in the same office space. Soon I began taking on my own coaching work and co-facilitating workshops with other TCI partners. Over time we began working on projects directly together. We found a rhythm in designing client interventions or leadership programs and then delivering the work together.

One of my favorite things about this phase of our work, especially when we were both up-front starting a new workshop, was to see how long it would take before clients would ask: "Are you two married?" We would slip something into our introductions about taking the dogs out that morning or why it took so long to get a cup of coffee, just to have fun with each other and the group. I loved how we became great thinking partners together and then how we found ourselves immersed with each other in work, play, downtime, social time and every other facet of life together. We found a "oneness" in our relationship that just kept bringing us closer together.

I know what unconditional love is because Kathy came into my life. I know what it feels like to love another without holding back a single ounce of myself because of her.

Kathy and I shared the depth of our love for each other by exchanging greeting cards. Over the course of holidays, anniversaries and other special or ordinary occasions, there were hundreds of them: cards plus faxes, poems and letters to each other. After Kathy's death in 2016, I gathered them to create a view of our love story. I started looking for themes and then combining the various pieces to see what version of our story might emerge.

In the next few chapters, my intention is to first and foremost honor the incredible love story that became our life together, our "one wild and precious life," as described in this excerpt from "The Summer Day," one of our favorite Mary Oliver poems:

The Summer Day
by Mary Oliver

"I don't know exactly what a prayer is.
I do know how to pay attention,
how to fall down into the grass,
how to kneel down in the grass,
how to be idle and blessed,
how to stroll through the fields,
which is what I have been doing all day.

Tell me, what else should I have done?
Doesn't everything die at last, and too soon?

Tell me . . . what is it YOU plan to do
with your one wild and precious life?"[2]

2 "The Summer Day" from *HOUSE OF LIGHT* by Mary Oliver, published by Beacon Press, Boston. Copyright © 1990 by Mary Oliver, used herewith by permission of the Charlotte Sheedy Literary Agency, Inc http://www.beacon.org/House-of-Light-P367.aspx

• CHAPTER 3 •

Our "WE" Comes to Life

With all my heart John Davis –

Our WE is Magic

Our Love is Grand and such a special blessing . . . full of life, possibilities, peace and laughter!

Divine through and through

I do love you!

Kathryn D.

Kathy Cramer –

How is it that my world came to intersect with your world and now, every day, there is OUR world . . . the world of our WE.

How is it that my heart jumps and my entire being tingles at your loving touch . . . ?

How is it that I get to be the one celebrating YOU in this very moment . . . ?

My heart is full of love
My spirit is full of wonder
And all of me is full of celebration of YOU . . .
Every day I feel so grateful
and every day I feel so blessed
for home
for work
for love
for our WE
and most of all, for you.

I am so thankful that you and our WE are in my life and I am celebrating all that is YOU and every way you show-up. I love you,

John

OUR LIFE TOGETHER WAS indeed precious, and as I look back and take-in some of the details I found in our notes and letters to each other, it makes my heart sing once again.

The expressions of our shared love were endless, yet a number of themes always seemed to be present. Early in our time together, there was a realization that the relationship was taking on an undeniable identity in and of itself. As the two of us grew closer and began the process of intentionally creating a life together, our oneness took on the designation of our WE. There was each one of us individually a part of the relationship and then there was the two of us together–that was our "WE". She was a gift to me, I was a gift to her, and from that, our WE arose, a palpable part of our everyday living.

Then we always talked about "holding each other with an open hand". This was an expression of our unconditional love for each other, as we insisted always that the other be just who they are and that we would not hold onto the other in any constraining manner.

And we always saw our relationship as a dance, each of us able to be in-step with the other on so many levels. We loved the times of literally getting to dance with each other at weddings or parties or for a while as members of a dance-supper club. We also had this thing we called "knee dancing," that would happen most often when we would run into each other in the kitchen, and we would spontaneously go into some knee-to-knee dance moves!

I loved our life together. I love Kathryn with all my heart. We were so very intentional about creating a life that was filled with unconditional love—for each other, ourselves, and for all the family and friends we had in our life. While there were a number of other themes in our writing to each other, I will share some details on those above to illustrate what it meant to look at life always through love and to be willing to continue life, no matter what transition changes the form of that love.

I BELIEVE

I believe in our hopes and dreams.

I believe in you, me, us.

I believe that what we have together is precious.

I believe in the sun, moon, and stars to guide us and keep us.

And I believe you're the best thing that's ever happened to me.

I love you.

Please take all of this message in Johndavis, especially this part:

"You're the BEST thing that's ever happened to me."

Thank you for choosing me and "WE".

I am so lucky, I can't believe how lucky.

With all my love,

KDC

Kath –

To say your name, Kathryn, and your name as my wife and lover,

all in the same sentence gives me, my body & my "I",

chills, thrills & . . . eagerness.

Feel me eager to find you.

Feel me eager to find our WE.

Feel me eager for you to find me.

Then,

Feel the warmth of my breath on your neck.

Feel the softness of my kiss on your lips.

Feel the fierceness of my love & desire for you, KDC.
Feel me saying with my all:
I do
I will
I am
From the depths of my heart and the vastness of my soul,
I am loving you Kathryn, and I love our WE with all of who I am.
John

KATHY AND I DATED for three years before we were married on August 1, 1998. Our life together unfolded from that point with such joy, possibility and creativity. We never stopped being in love. Actually, we kept falling deeper in love. Kathy always made it clear how much she wanted me to just be the person I am, and I was asking the same of her. That depth of unconditional love was continuously a new place for each of us. It was the foundation from which our life, our "WE" could grow each day and every day

I have to admit when we first started talking about our "WE," it was hard to exactly understand the concept. However, as our relationship grew and began to truly flourish, it became evident that what we were experiencing was indeed beyond just the two of us as individuals living the life of a married couple. I can't say it any more simply than it was an experience of oneness.

What really brought our WE home for me was how we began to be experienced out in the world. I think part of it was how "in-synch" we were with each other and part of it was how that translated to how others would describe being with the two of us. They could sense and feel our deep level of alignment – not an agreement on everything – but a soul-level connection that was palpable. And as Kathy and I began to understand that our WE was actually having an impact, it brought us closer together and allowed us a chance to be deliberate in how we were present with others.

I don't remember that we talked openly about the concept of our WE with others, yet the two of us were very open in exploring what our collective WE was creating in the world and extending the love between us outwards.

Kathy seemed to always find a way to acknowledge and say thank you for the world we were creating everyday. She was clear about helping me know that she experienced my heart feeling her joy and pain and fears and aspirations. She loved helping me know how my mind could join with hers in bringing new ideas and processes to people who want to grow and excel and contribute to the world.

She would say thank you for what she described as my generous, deep spirit that could give her life, my own life and our life together meaning. I knew she loved being my wife. I knew she loved me for who I am.

Dear Johndavis . . .

Happy Easter.

Fifteen years ago, I faxed you a love letter on Easter from Italy – Lake Como. I went there by myself to get some R&R after [my brother] Dan's death. I was then - and am now – very much in love with you.

This Easter I keep remembering the "photographs for God" that I took when my Mom died and when I saw my Dad dead in his bed 6 weeks later. These images feel so final . . . and of course represent their transitions beyond this life to who knows what kind of adventure! I do feel each of their spirits with me and with us.

I want to thank you again for your generous love of Mom and Dad. You made them laugh. You gave them such respect and kindness. You were there for them as they struggled and prepared to let go of the lives they created for themselves together. I really believe that they both hated to leave us . . . our WE, you and me.

WE did an amazing job of reassuring them that our love for each other is strong and big enough to hold them, and Emily and Nadia [my daughter and granddaughter], and both of our whole families. We showed them a devotion and commitment to each other that is deep and abiding. Our "WE" held them close when they needed to be held more than ever before.

Johndavis I want to love you better and better and better in moments of anxiety. I am so sorry for letting you down when I feel hurt. I am so thrilled to be your wife at all times – even in our disconnected moments of sadness. Thank you for creating this life with me . . . for loving [our home at] #65 . . . for reaching out for [our Innsbrook lake house] #2232 . . . for working in the most wonderful work together . . . for loving our family and friends and [our dogs] Sophie and Gracie together.

I am saying "Yes" to you and to all of this and more . . . I can't imagine what we will cook-up next, and I know it will be created out of our love . . . the love that inspires me every morning, noon and night to be more and more alive!

Feel me loving you Johndavis and feel me loving our "WE."

This Easter and every one to come.

Kathryn D.

• CHAPTER 4 •

Holding Her with an Open Hand

The Truelove
by David Whyte

There is a faith in loving fiercely
the one who is rightfully yours,
especially if you have
waited years and especially
if part of you never believed
you could deserve this
loved and beckoning hand
held out to you this way.

. . . and you will
walk across any territory
and any darkness,
however fluid and however

dangerous, to take the
one hand you know
belongs in yours.[3]

Kathy and I never expected to find each other, much less create a life together. We had never met until that day at my office, our lives had never crossed paths, nor had our circles of friends ever intersected. Yet, as our relationship developed it became clear that we did belong together. The depth of the love, the quality of the love and the ease with which we fell in love, all told us we were meant for each other. However, there was work at the beginning of the relationship for each of us to get to that point of knowing we did belong together. I had been adamant that I didn't want to entertain a new relationship after my separation. Kathy was trying to trust these feelings of love that for her had sprung up rather quickly. We each would talk about these doubts and try to be there for the other to learn more about what we were really feeling and experiencing. There was an openness that we nurtured so as to ensure we knew what was in each other's heart.

---

3 Printed with permission from Many Rivers Press, www.davidwhyte.com. "The Truelove," by David Whyte, from *The House of Belonging*, ©Many Rivers Press, Langley, WA, USA. https://davidwhyte.com

Dear John Stephen Davis –

I have known and loved you for all these years and never once before have I been so in love with you. How could that be? All these years you've been holding me with your open hands.

I was as deeply in love with you as possible – in fact I was bursting with LOVE – the first night you followed me to Innsbrook. Way back then I tried to tell myself to slow down . . . wait and see . . . keep experiencing, so you will know what is real and what is pure desire.

Day in and day out, month after month, year by year I see you and feel you and lay beside you and listen to you and watch you dance with the world . . . and know that this love story is real!

We are creating story after story that takes my breath away and surrounds me. Our stories make love to the world. Thank you for being my husband John. I am so excited to be your wife.

All my love, all my life!

Kathryn D.

DAVID WHYTE'S POEM "THE Truelove" captured some of what we were feeling and came to serve as an inspiration early in our relationship. We could each relate to the idea in Whyte's words of going through whatever life presented in order to find that true love. And to then be able to clearly take the "one hand that belongs in yours". I began to tell Kathy that "I am holding you close, but with an open hand." At that time, this was my way, and then our way of saying to each other that I am committed to you and if, at some point, you find our relationship is not working then you are truly free to decide to move on to what's next.

As we realized our relationship was indeed one that we would be in for the long run, that expression really came to mean that I am holding you close, while at the same time, I want you to be who you truly are as a person, not who I might want you to be. It was our way to acknowledge and nurture the actual experience of unconditional love.

Over the years there were so many variations of how we would remind each other of this core principle of "holding you with an open hand". It never wavered and in fact grew stronger, particularly as it took on the meaning that we wanted each other to always be our authentic selves.

Dear Johndavis,
I am learning and growing so much as your Best Friend, Lover, Partner and Wife.
This year has been one of transition, dreams and aspirations.

You are changing, I am changing.
We are changing together – all at once – for the better.
Can you feel me loving you and holding on for whatever may be around the bend,
while we make up the life (and lives) we want?
You do hold my heart in your open hands.
I do Love you –
Kathryn D.

Kathryn
Feel my hand beckoning to yours,
Feel it close around you and hold you near.
Feel the strength in the holding
and notice it is done with an open hand.
My hand will always be open to you . . .
I am loving you Kathryn,
John

IT WAS SOMEWHERE AROUND 2005 that Kathy began a new writing project that was basically aimed at codifying her approach to the consulting work she and those at The Cramer Institute used in all the client leadership work. What she coached her clients on was making positive shifts in the way they saw themselves, others, and their situations so that they leverage the richness of their experiences. There were many discussions on what could be used to name this work and be used as a title for her new book. That is when Asset-Based Thinking® (ABT) was introduced and went on to become the topic of four new books. The title of the first book in the series became, *Change the Way You See Everything, through Asset-Based Thinking®*, although it took many iterations to settle on that name. It was during that time that one of my cards to her included the following expression of yet another facet of holding her with an open hand.

> *Kathryn –*
> *Your new book title may still be in question and yet this is one that is clear & locked in:*
> My Open Heart, *and it has been permanently checked out in your name.*
> My Open Heart *tells the story of what your deep abiding love can do to my soul. It tells the story of what it is like to be holding onto that love forever and holding you all along with an open hand.*
> My Open Heart *truly is the story of how my soul connects, grows and expands because of the presence of YOU in my life and your love that holds me just as I am.*
> *As we continue to write OUR story, know that it will unfold as a timeless classic – and it truly is a rare edition, one that I hope every couple can find.*
> *Having found you Kath, I am here forever.*

I love you dearly,
John

Our words to each other certainly speak for themselves. In sharing them I hope the significance of who we were together, what we experienced together, and the life we literally created together jumps off the page and touches the hearts of anyone reading these words. And on the chance that a heart is touched, my hope is it will bring the realization that each day choices can be made within our lives to create the story we so long for ourselves.

CHAPTER 5

Our Dance

EARLY IN OUR MARRIAGE we decided that every 5 years we would do an "official" photo shoot to commemorate that anniversary. It was a way to be intentional about marking the passage of time within the relationship by capturing visual images of us as a couple. It was also a chance to pause and reflect on what we had experienced together the previous five years. It couldn't help but include looking forward at what we wanted to create together next.

With good friends a couple of years before our tenth anniversary, we made a trip to Santa Fe and spent an entire weekend roaming through the art galleries there. We discovered the artist Randall Hasson[4] who had a unique technique of weaving text into the visual elements of his paintings, using his own style of calligraphy. We bought one of his pieces of a young girl playing in the sand that included a poem by Rumi.

4 https://randallmhasson.com/the-dance/

As our tenth anniversary grew closer, we started discussing the up-coming commemorative photo shoot. We somehow came upon the idea to commission a painting by Hasson of the two of us.

It was a really fun process to help him understand our story, our history of writing to each other and some of what we loved . . . including how much fun we always had on the dance floor. Through a series of interviews, Randall found his inspiration:

"The Dance" ©2009 Randall M. Hasson, Acrylic on Canvas

His website includes the following description:

"Private commission for John Davis and author Kathryn Cramer, PhD on the occasion of their 10th wedding anniversary. The text in the painting contains writing from their love letters and "The Truelove," a poem by

David Whyte contained in their wedding vows. Kathryn is the author of numerous books on Asset-Based Thinking® and a founding partner in the company, The Cramer Institute."

IN THE PREVIOUS CHAPTER, I introduced David Whyte's poem, "The Truelove" and with his permission, Randall included it as part of the calligraphy he captured in our painting. It was significant for us because we had used part of the words from the poem in our wedding vows, along with the already discussed part of holding the hand that belongs.

The commissioning process started early in the year of anniversary #10 and the finished painting was delivered very close to our actual August 1st anniversary date. We were beyond excited to unveil it in each other's presence. These were my words in one of the cards I gave her that day:

Kathryn,

As you look for the first time at THE DANCE, notice the exquisite joy in both our faces. Notice how we hold each other with an open hand. Notice what our version of "loving fiercely", is present on the canvas.

And, most of all, notice that right now I am reaching out to pull you close, as we move into the next steps of our Dance!

Happy Anniversary, Kathryn,
Love, John

About a year later, Kathy made a trip to Chicago a few days ahead of my being able to join her there to visit our friends Nicole and Eric. I was delaying my part of the trip for a work assignment and to continue conversations and some parenting-type work with my son Adam and my daughter Emily. They were each going through their own parenting challenges, as well as work related difficulties. I was so fortunate to be able to have the in-depth talks that we found possible by then.

Kathy, too, had become a trusted resource and both my kids embraced her into their lives. Even with all that love and acceptance, she had had a tough challenge winning over their hearts in the beginning. Back then, both kids were still reeling from the impact of my divorce from their mom. Today, they will both tell you of the huge impact Kathy had and has on their lives. She was able to hold them where they were, while helping them see themselves in new ways over the years. Kathy embraced Adam and Emily's children as if they were her own grandchildren. She became their "Kackie," and they were showered with that same depth of love the rest of us felt from her.

Alone in our bedroom at home after Kathy had left for Chicago, I was looking at our painting now hanging above the fireplace and I sent these words in a note that night to Kathy:

Kathryn,
Earlier today I found myself standing in front of our painting of THE DANCE.
It makes me smile each time I see it.

I smile because of what we did to create the actual piece of art itself.
I smile because we look like we are meant to be dancing together always.
I smile because we get to do the dancing amongst those "double delight" roses.

And the smile that lingers longer, comes from knowing first-hand what it was like to experience your written words to me in our early years. Words that now are part of this painting.

I remember the anticipation of wondering when the next fax would arrive.
I remember the joy found in the connecting we were creating.

And I remember getting lost (as in completely swept off my feet), with you as I was writing my letters to you.
As I stood before our painting, in that moment of smiling in our bedroom, I realized I wanted to connect with you through a letter since we are missing each other in the travel schedules. As we spoke on the phone before you met Eric & Nicole, I was feeling you reach out to touch my heart once again. I feel the warmth of your embrace and the incredible energy in the love you send my way – and to the world.

I am in love with you, and I am in love with the life we are creating together.

I feel your support for me personally & I feel the tremendous support you offer to Emily & Adam – and to me as I work through all that stuff. I find myself getting really excited when I start talking about ABT (Asset-Based Thinking®) with a group, especially when I get to tell them we are married.

It is a thrill and an honor to be part of your positive conspiracy. I can't wait to find out what we conspire to do together next. I most of all can't wait to see you, feel you, hold you and kiss you (and . . .) on Sunday evening.

Enjoy your weekend, come rain or shine and know that I am on my way soon to find you.

I love you Kathryn,
John

It was surprising the way we found ourselves working on the commissioning project for our tenth anniversary "photo shoot". It came rather quickly in the calls with the artist that the metaphor of dance was such a beautiful reflection of the time we had together up to that point in our relationship.

Because of his use of calligraphy within the painting, we had a great time exploring our writing to each other to offer ideas on what might be included. The theme of our "WE" jumped out right away as well and became central to the other quotes Randall included.

"Celebrating our WE" was beautifully scripted across the entire painting. It speaks to the entirety of the life we created together. It offers a message of what can happen when two people remain so completely themselves yet dive so deeply into a relationship. The dance of going from me to us to WE and all that brought along the way, helped create a life I could have never imagined otherwise.

THE DANCING GOES ON . . . AND ON

We saw our life together as a creative dance all along the way. This dance included the freedom of expressing our love for the next home we would find and furnish to the client work together to the ways we would embrace family and friends. Yes, there were the times on the literal dance floor and now as I look back I see how each day we would, in some way, find ourselves dancing with life. These next writings we shared show that, each in their own way, and bring me yet one more time of realizing the depth and breadth of our life's "dance card".

My Husband . . .

He's the man who touches my heart like no other.
He helps to make life worthwhile.
I can turn to him in good times and in bad times when I need comfort, reassurance, or a smile to warm my heart.

He's my lover, partner, companion, and friend.

He's the man who makes my dreams come true. He's the one who dances with me throughout our days and into the nights. The most wonderful thing about my life is having a husband like you – someone to share with, someone to dream with. . .

And on Father's Day, I wanted to say "thank you" for all the things you have done to bring joy and love to our family. My Mom and Dad felt so loved by you Johndavis! As do Andy, Karina, Jamie, Ali, Jan and Emily, Nadi, Adam, Tamra, Rose, Jaden and Jaxon . . . a "Baker's Dozen" for sure (not to mention your Barbara, Susan, Tim, and everyone in their families).

You are love & joy embodied . . . and I do love your body!

Kathryn D.

Kathy –

The greatest gift you keep on giving me is that of accepting me just as I am. From that place of freedom to be me, I get to keep growing. I always feel your support – and encouragement – to go deeper into my exploration.

You always rejoice with me as I learn something new about myself. You continuously help me expand my view of myself. All of this allows me to grow while at the same time, it enables our WE to grow.

Come with me to find even more ways for us to grow together. Come dance with me to the new music we are sure to find. Come with me into the next phase and then the next and then the next . . .

And in this moment, feel me holding you close and asking once again . . . will you be my Valentine, forever?

I love you,
John

Kathy could create such beautiful poems, inspiring words and heartfelt sentiments. As I close out the examples of how we saw our life together as a dance in so many ways, following is one expression I can keep coming back to for a true glimpse of her love:

Dear Johndavis!
You are such a "Loooovely Man"....

Will you dance with me to the beat of your drum?

Will you hold me close and never let me go?

Will you let me hold you close and never let you go?

Will you look into the mirror everyday and know
your face – your eyes – your smile is the one I love
and the one I fall in love with every day?

Two Step and Tango

Here we come!

Love you

Kathy

We actually never officially learned the Two Step but did take Tango lessons for a minute! In a big remodeling project, we built an island in the new kitchen that had a lot of room around all four sides. We would use that space to try out our dance moves in those last few years together. Inevitably we would wind up sitting in the bay window looking out at the beautiful patio and pool and just holding each other in amazement of all that we had together.

• CHAPTER 6 •

When The Writing Stopped

John Davis
I am so thrilled to be "forevering" with you.
I can't imagine a life, my life, without you by my side.
What a gift you are. I can't wait to see what we cook up next . . . and next . . . and next!

FOREVER we will be creating, won't we? Because that is what we do – we "make it all up as we go." And just look at what has already shown up (in the homes we have created) . . .Stratford, Ridgetop, Westminster Place, 2629, #65 and 2232. . .Whew what a joy to be with You!

Kathy loves John!
Kathy is in love with John.

Our life together was so full. Full of work, family, friends, travel, goofing-off, daily walks and endless ways of loving each other. Especially after I retired from my corporate career and joined Kathy in working at The Cramer Institute, we found ourselves loving the added depth we had created for being together. Every facet of our lives was a shared experience, and it was from that place of joy, we found ourselves easily talking about how we would be together forever.

It was simply a given fact. The sweet entanglement we had created was a surprise, a continuous blessing and statement of what we both wanted for the rest of our lives. That hope, that plan and that reality was spoken of in many different ways. Our relationship was bound to last forever.

And then there was the diagnosis.

A check-up and mammogram in January of 2015 turned into an ultrasound that turned into more tests that then took the final turn into a confirmed diagnosis of stage 4 breast cancer. What's more the cancer had metastasized to Kathy's bones and liver. After an unbelievably hard day in conversation with the medical oncologist, the radiation oncologist, and the surgeon about options and plans, we left the hospital with heads spinning, hearts hurting, and spirits shattered.

Kathy's response to all of it was something that I still hear with awe and amazement: "Yes and now what?"

Yes, I have been diagnosed with cancer. And so now what shall my response be? What shall we do to carry on with our lives? It was such a classic Kathy response, born out of her life view and her inspirational approach to daily living.

The treatment plan was established, and we went back to the hospital for the first day of chemo, expecting to be there for the several hours the infusions would require. However, her oncologist took us into her office and began explaining an alternative. The FDA had just approved a new oral chemo treatment and Kathy fit the eligibility criteria to be able to start using it. Her doctor had run the clinical trials in St. Louis and intimately knew its capability. She was strongly encouraging Kathy to move to that treatment protocol. It really didn't seem like a hard decision; however, it did take some effort to get it approved through insurance as it was a very expensive bottle of pills. In addition to the pills would be weekly injections and eventually some targeted radiation treatments later on after the tumors were reduced in size. And so it began.

For the next year, Kathy would sit at the breakfast table, drink her coffee, eat her eggs, take her pills and announce, "well that's my chemo treatment for today." She knew how fortunate she was to be getting this form of treatment. There was no hair loss, no extended fatigue, and only some occasional nausea that seemed to pass in a day or so. After several months the doctor showed her how the tumors were slowly being reduced!

The limited side effects let Kathy maintain her lifestyle essentially as if things were normal. She kept her physical fitness routines pretty much the same–workouts in the gym, walks in the neighborhood and swimming in the pool as weather allowed. She kept her relentless work schedule in place and kept her many initiatives with clients and colleagues moving forward. Our social calendar didn't change too much either. Dinners with friends and family, a few trips out of town for fun and our usual weekend downtime at the lake house. To the outside world she appeared to be the same Kathy we all knew and loved. To the outside world, our WE was as strong and present as ever. And that was even more true between the two of us–it all brought us even closer together as a couple.

Part of what everyone knew about Kathy was her positive attitude about life. It is actually too narrow a description to call it just a "positive attitude". The truth was she had a way of seeing the good in herself, in others and in all of what life brought her way. She had a way of helping all of us reframe our own perceptions and judgments about things to bring out the possibilities that were otherwise hidden. These innate character traits served her so well throughout her time in treatment. It allowed her to not dwell on the negative side of possibilities. It allowed her to never fear the worst of what could happen or even entertain the possibility of that for too long. That made it all the easier for me and others close to her to not carry a burden of fear over what might happen next. When she received that confirming diagnosis and had the immediate response "yes and now what", I was able to join her in rolling up my sleeves and doing all that was needed to take the next step and then the next.

John -
I can be with you . . . in our dreams
in our days & nights
in our work
in our friendship
in our families
in our Life
I cannot be without you . . . ever again in this life and in the next.

Because I am You
You are Me
We are WE
Kathryn D.

Yes, she had her worries and doubts at times and that was when I found myself doing all I could to be there for her as an active listener. I was always watching for those small signs and encouraging her to speak openly when she had a dark moment. There weren't that many, honestly, and that enabled me to stand even stronger in supporting her. Knowing so many spouses who had to become true care-givers in similar situations, I knew how fortunate I was.

Kathy made a conscious choice early on to limit the number of people with whom she would discuss her diagnosis and treatment progress. I was to find out later the list of those who had no idea she had cancer was much longer than I ever expected. It was her wish to handle it in her way and it was all good for her as a result.

By almost every measure you might look at during her treatment, she was essentially "normal"—she just also happened to be battling stage 4 cancer. Then, slowly it became evident she was beginning to beat it. The cancer on her bones began to clear and the lump in her breast reduced to the point where they were able to surgically remove what was left. She went into radiation treatment to finish off the small tumors left on the liver. After a year of pills and the other treatments, her doctor declared that she was being placed in the "remission" group. It was a day of huge relief.

We decided to take a trip to the Gulf in early March of 2016 and spend a week on the beach to just relax away with the good news and do a reset for what we wanted to be next. On that trip we started talking about shifting our work schedules to deliberately take more time away, we imagined for three-four weeks at a time. We figured out how we would be able to arrange our respective client loads to accommodate those kinds of getaways. We left feeling energized about making our lifestyle changes. When we got home, we had an unsolicited offer to buy our house. While that hadn't been part of our plan, we quickly decided it was a fit with our new intentions. We had a contract to sell our house by early April, purchased a new house by the end of April and completed the move-in at the end of May.

Then . . . it was a Monday morning in late June and we had just come off a busy weekend of hosting our first two dinner parties in our new home. Kathy had started writing a new book intended to help others navigate big health related challenges and was feverishly working on getting the book proposal finished to submit to her editor, when her doctor called. Before jumping in her car, she repeated her doctor's instructions to me as she was scrambling to wrap-up the proposal cover letter: "Get to the ER right now, your kidney function numbers are not right." The lab results, just in from the previous week's tests, then set in motion a whirlwind of activity at the hospital that turned out to be the beginning of the end.

AND THEN THE WRITING ACTUALLY STOPPED

I DON'T REMEMBER THE actual last time we exchanged cards or written notes with each other before that day at the end of June when she went into the hospital. There were always the endless ones left on a pillow, stuck onto a computer, wedged into the console of the car or handed to each other while teaching a workshop together. We were always writing these love notes to each other. It was just another way of how we expressed our unending and undying–unconditional–love for each other.

Then, on July 13, 2016, the writing stopped.

That was the day Kathy died from the breast cancer that had rapidly reappeared on her liver. She was at the peak of her career; we were at the peak of being in love, and it all disappeared. She had been in treatment for over fifteen months, had even been placed in the "remission" group, and then in a matter of three weeks the cancer came roaring back and consumed her liver. I can't even remember the last conversation Kathy and I had, as everything was such a blur at the end.

The speed with which the end came, the way it all happened so quickly, neither she nor I, nor those around us, had a chance to even consider that she was about to die. On what turned out to be her last day, when the doc took me aside to inform me there was nothing that could be done, my world came to an abrupt standstill.

That same ICU doctor then, in a gesture of pure compassion, allowed family and friends to come be with Kathy, for what turned out to be the last six hours of her life. She was unconscious but responding in subtle ways to the endless expressions of love. The doctor kept saying, "she can hear everything you say to her."

Being able to witness the flow of family and friends show up and be with Kathy, was a gift of great significance for me. As they were seeking their own way to grapple with the unbelievable scene they found, I too was searching for mine. Their expressions of love penetrated my heart and have been a sustained system of support since then.

That direct support continued through the funeral services and for several weeks beyond. It was essential for my being able to sustain the energy and focus to deal with losing Kathy. The pace of all that happened, the magnitude of what was required, and the uncharted territory it represented for me, made it an all-consuming time.

Then I found myself truly alone–me and the puppies by ourselves in a new house that had barely started becoming a home. All of a sudden that house seemed way too big, out of proportion for just us and way too empty now that everyone had left . . . especially Kathy. That reality hit me hard and that was when I knew my life was totally altered forever, that my 3rd Life had ended, and I was facing yet one more new lifetime.

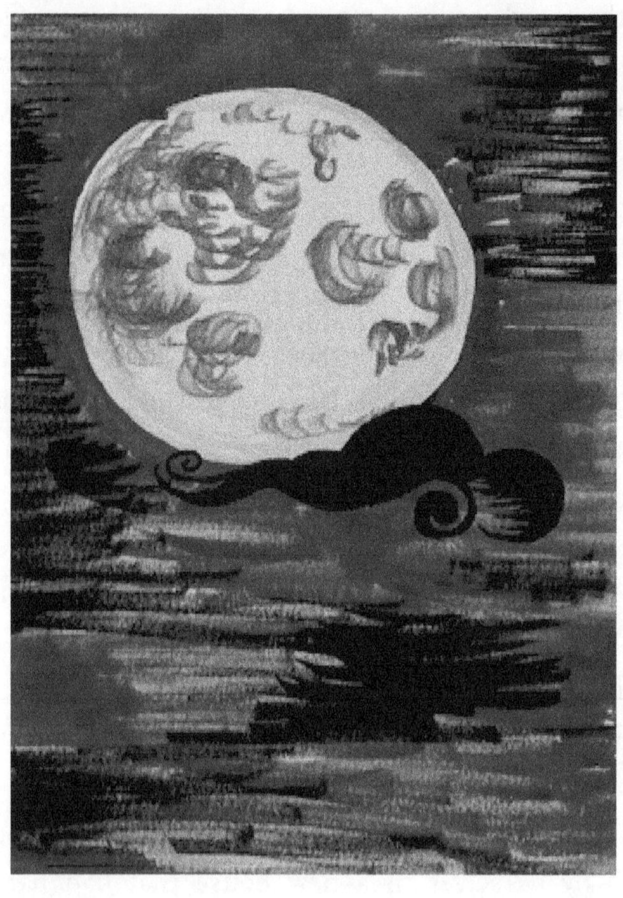

Original artwork by Rosemary Renee' Davis - ©2021

Lifetime #3 Perspectives

MY EXPERIENCE OF LOVE

LIFETIME #3 WAS A lifetime experience in love, as well as a lifetime of being in love. The early expression of that love came in our saying to each other "I am holding you with an open hand." That expression of being willing to "let go" early on turned into a life of accepting each other and loving each other unconditionally. The discovery of our "WE" happened between us and beyond us. I am still surprised at how our "oneness" was experienced by others as WE were out in the world. What a privilege to know the love between us spilled out so clearly into the world around us.

Kathy gave me the life-changing gift of being loved completely for just who I am. Being loved in such an unconditional way moved me to loving myself as never before. Yes, I have always held some knowing of a love for myself, but Kathy's love enabled me to see and love myself in a completely different way.

Self-love jumped to the forefront when I said yes to my heart in those earliest days of our relationship. I remember so well the moment I gave myself permission to admit I was falling in love and how amazing that felt. The subsequent flow of Kathy's love for me only accelerated my sense of self and my ability to love myself. There was such an ease of being totally open about loving each other throughout this lifetime and that then allowed a new level of acceptance and love of myself.

MY EVOLUTION IN CONSCIOUSNESS

Being loved so completely by Kathy allowed me to gain so much self-awareness and with that find new levels of my own consciousness. As I began to appreciate myself more deeply, I was also able to see and appreciate those around me with new eyes.

That appreciation helped fuel my desire to help others in their own self-awareness. When I began my work at The Cramer Institute, I made the conscious choice to bring that intention to my coaching and group work. It was my attempt to elevate my and others' consciousness by helping them learn more about who they are and gain new understandings of what they bring to the world.

That intention came from the realization in my second lifetime that for things in the world to get better, we would collectively have to move to a higher level of consciousness, one where we could accept each other as we are and that enables us to see each other through the eyes of compassion, care, and unconditional love.

"Seeing another" plays out in a beautiful way in one of my workshops where I do something I call coaching in real time. This happens in the context of helping an individual find their voice and gain a greater sense of their personal power and presence in front of a group. At the end of that coaching experience, I go to the front of the room and speak in private to the person, while the rest of the group prepares some written feedback. Inevitably, when I am speaking with the individual, I can look into their eyes and get a sense of their soul. I believe that is because they have been willing to be vulnerable... and I have been willing to be totally present with them. Gaining an understanding of this over several years has clearly been another way of adding to my understanding of consciousness.

My third lifetime gave me the experience of living every day in the consciousness that is unconditional love. I now know that it was about leading and preparing me for the work—with myself and with others—that was to come next.

A MOMENT TO REFLECT . . . ON LIFETIME #3

I AM BEYOND GRATEFUL for the life Kathy and I shared, and the love that defined our time together. The ease of it all and the chance to always be "making it up together" made it such a beautiful time.

I am blessed by the many ways I was able to grow because of being held in Kathy's unconditional love. That growth spilled into my own sense of self-love and the acceptance of being just who I am.

I am still shocked it all came to an end and yet trust there is a greater purpose being served for her and me. I know that I have the essence of Kathy with me each day and that she knows I love her with all my heart, even in her absence.

I hold all that we had together clearly in my heart each day, each moment and it brings me to a place of joy and thanksgiving each time I pause to remember. And you know one of those most consistent times of remembering comes whenever I hear Eric Clapton singing, "You Are Wonderful Tonight"!!

Wherever you are in the universe today Kath, I feel you here in the depths of my being and in this heart that is very open to you, very open to me and so very open to my new world.

Original heartwork by Jaxon Wesley Davis - ©2021

Lifetime #3.5 - Navigating the Pain of a Lost Love

Kathy was gone and as the reality of my new circumstances sunk in, I eventually had to face the cold hard fact of having to live my life every day in some (new) normal way. I quickly realized that meant carrying on as a regular human being, as a working person and even more, as someone in a whole lot of pain from loss. This was clearly a new phase for me, but it felt like a real in-between place. I was in no shape to literally start life anew and I eerily felt I was still living in my old life. Or at least wanted that to be true. That's why it felt like this was Lifetime #3.5 - something not the same as #3, yet I was not ready for #4.

I did not really know how to grieve, yet I did know I wanted to be conscious about my grieving. My attempts at doing so included giving in to the many feelings of loss, sadness, hurt, anger, pain and whatever else showed up and then trying my best to let them flow through me. I knew that holding them back would only bring more to work through later.

Part of my process to let my feelings flow turned into writing. Whenever I felt the pain of the loss I put pen to paper (or fingers to keyboard) and let the words show up. It helped me to get it out and it surprised me what did show up. Part of my surprise continues to be how much it takes to process the significance of a loss.

I started writing then through a blogging outlet I called "My Open Heart," as my way of opening to and moving through a very intentional process of grieving. Writing about what I was experiencing and feeling, and trying to understand it all, was relatively easy for me. You'll see excerpts of my writing during this time throughout the next few chapters. Often my writing was in the form of letters to Kathy, a continuation of our long-held tradition. The writing was always free flow, in the moment. I was an open vessel of expression, pouring out what was tugging at my heart, heavy in my heart, or blocking my way to an open heart.

The words seemed to come without thinking, they just would show up on the page as long as I could stay open and present. The hard part was moving to share those words beyond my own private journal. The sharing began as an act of faith, in that I had (and have) no real idea of any impact my sharing may have on others. I do know there was something liberating for me in the willingness to share openly. It allowed me the chance to more easily find what was in my heart. Through the willingness to say it out loud as if others were listening, it helped me find myself. It brought my inner thoughts into the world and put me in a place of accountability and intentionality. As you shall see, being intentional has become a very important theme for me.

As I look back over all that writing, I now see a number of key themes that emerged:

- My choosing to grieve in a conscious way, even with not knowing how to really deal with the pain of loss.
- How I never imagined a life without Kathy and my longing to have it back again. The anger in feeling "It wasn't supposed to be this way" and "Now what am I going to do?" And then hearing Kathy's words: "Yes... and now what"?
- The challenge I faced in "letting go" in order to "move forward".
- Finding a transformational sense of strength emerge that ultimately enabled a clear sense of moving forward.
- My realization that we (Kathy and I) are always together in spirit and have a heart-connection that will never go away. My acknowledgment of

the gift of unconditional love that Kathy brought into my life.

THERE IS ALSO AN interesting facet of the writing that became evident, only in looking back over it the 4+ years since I began writing. I found in a number of the pieces written, I had been able to "offer" myself guidance and some deeper wisdom that was important in key moments to help me push through a difficult time. I smile now as I know it was actually wisdom coming through me, not from me. So, I say thank you, from a very grateful heart, to my guides, angels, loved ones and even Kathy herself, for being with me in those ways at some critical points in facing my grief.

I hope that in sharing my experience and this wisdom, others in their own grieving process may find some hope in moving through their own experiences of loss. No matter the cause of the loss.

Original artwork by Rosemary Renee' Davis - ©2021

• CHAPTER 7 •

Choosing to Grieve

THE MOMENT OF WITNESSING Kathy take her last breath will be a scene forever etched in my memory. My daughter Emily, Kathy's nephew Jamie, and two good friends, Robyn and Bob, were present in the room at the time. We looked at each other in disbelief, we embraced . . . and we wept. Kathy was gone.

What is hard to remember is all that happened in the next few weeks after Kathy died. It was a painful blur, filled with so many "have-to" activities and obligations dealing with "estate" stuff. I was on automatic pilot and fortunately was surrounded by family and friends, helping me navigate the aftermath. My writing started during that time somewhere along the way.

I tried to make sense of a life without Kathy, but there was no way any of it made any sense at all to me. We had been in the middle of re-imagining a new phase of life together, one that simply did not allow for the turn that had so rudely shown up. I had not ever imagined a life without Kathy Cramer in it. And then there it was, I had it. My sadness was overwhelming. My loss was real and deep.

I knew working through all of this grief would be a big process. I accepted that and I embraced what it had to bring to me. I knew I had to stay open to its calling and be willing to dance with what showed up as a result.

I never knew how hard it could be to lose someone as close as Kathy was to me. I had lost my father and mother, but the grief did not take on the intensity that it did with Kathy's loss. It was so hard to accept that it happened and that she was no longer here. We had such great ideas for what we wanted to create as our next phase. We were right on the verge of stepping into that in such an intentional way.

Well, a next phase was certainly going to have to happen now . . . just not as planned. That's where the pain really got most intense. That's where the loss hit hardest and deepest. So, I sat with and experienced a hurt and pain like I have never known. Yet I remained so grateful for the depth of the love we shared and the caring and supportive relationship we enjoyed. When I stepped into that place it helped ease the pain.

Now, there was also a paradox of sorts, I was dealing with.

From my own out-of-body experiences (OBE's), I had come to realize that "I", the essence of who I am lives on, independent of what happens with my physical body. Said another way, the one that I experience as "me", my consciousness, my soul, does not change even after the physical body is gone. The soul lives on, which for me is the experience of my conscious self. It is the one I know as me, the one I experience as John.

Each time I've had an OBE, I felt no different in terms of my experience of the conscious me than when I was with my body. This has led me to the realization that we are more than our physical bodies and that "I" will not die when my body dies.

Coming to fully understand and believe this enabled me to release my own fear of dying because "I" will never really die. So, on that understanding, the essence of Kathy did not die either. She is no longer here in her physical presence; however, she lives on in her spiritual presence.

On July 13th, 2016, Kathy had a rebirth day, leaving this world, returning to the world of spirit and slipping back into the Collective Consciousness. I can only imagine the welcome she received as she made that transition.

It has been strangely peaceful to consider what that welcome must have been like and what she is experiencing now as a result. Holding that focus helped take me away from the deep sense of loss I felt without her being right here.

The fact that you are no longer here in physical form is still so surreal for me. It is still not easy to accept and it just doesn't seem that it could even be possible. When I can get clear in my mind, I am able to go back to a fundamental belief that I have developed that says we each choose the time we will leave the physical plane. You've made your choice. I do not like it. I do not believe it. I do not want to have to deal with it.

And here I am, sitting in this bed without you by my side. I trust you know that you left without a doubt of your being at the top of your game. I trust you know about every statement of impact that people have written or spoken or felt. If this is an example of "leaving on your own terms", then I get it and I see how that could be a part of this.

After writing those words I took a few minutes to sit with the deep sense of peace and love that surrounded me and swelled from within. I paused long enough to anchor the grace that was touching my heart. I allowed myself to feel it so deeply as to know it was as real as Kathy standing there next to me saying it out loud.

With a full heart, flowing tears, and my whole being shaking from being touched in that moment, a rising sense of hope and promise began to come over me.

I got up and stepped outside into the night air and felt like I was going to be swept into the heavens. I felt light and free and alive and grateful and lucky and joyful. Peace, quiet within, calm strength, clear thinking, a knowing, even more not-knowing and above all the excitement of being in love, feeling loved and giving my love freely. This was all a part of what Kathy and I have and had. It is and was the foundation of a life together that each day allowed me to open to the world with complete certainty of self.

Being loved unconditionally like Kathy offered me, was a gift of immense proportions, the gift of a lifetime. In the quiet of the morning that gift made itself known in a very visceral way. The energy in and around my body was palpable. It was something real and beautiful I could hold on to, even as I let go of the real and beautiful physical presence of Kathy on this earth.

I would ask each day, each time I was in the house . . . "Where are you Kathycramer?" And that morning, in that moment I knew she was right there by my side, filling me with the reminders of what we had. Helping me remember the enormity of the gift of life together we have shared.

Thank you for being willing to hold me in this way. Help me continue to move forward. Be with me this way when you can and are able. Whisper to me sometime and tell me a little bit about your new world. Let me have just a glimpse of your new reality.

What has surprised you the most?

What is the one thing you want all of us to know for sure?

What can you help us know about what we are up to here, without your physical presence?

I'm just asking and at the same time I am letting the questions go. Perhaps on another morning like this. Perhaps not. Either way, I will always know your love is with me and that I am sending mine to you. May we continue with this dance, with our dance, until we can be together in whatever way is next.

I love you Kathryn. I can feel your love in and around me and I am grateful . . .

I sat with the hurt and pain of loss on one hand and the knowing that Kathy lives on as her conscious self, on the other hand. And I wondered why the pain and hurt was so intense even in the face of this belief that all really was very well with Kathy.

THE DREAM

It was a long hallway with doors to outside areas along one side. My right-hand side. I was walking along, and Kathy caught my attention out of the corner of my eye.

I saw her standing there on the other side of a doorway. I opened the door and stepped out and she grabbed my hands, holding me at arm's length like we were starting to dance. I felt her energy and pulled her close and wrapped my arms around her.

As soon as I was holding her, she began to cry. I held her so very close and felt her sobbing throughout her whole body. She did not say anything, she cried even as I pulled her closer. All I could think was that I love this woman with all my heart.

And then the dream ended.

I woke up in shock because it was Kathy that was crying in my arms and not the other way around. I know how it hurts to not be able to hold her each day and my belief is that the place she is in knows no hurt nor pain nor sorrow, just love in the very deepest sense possible.

I let myself believe that her crying was the same reason as my crying, that she was missing me as much as I was missing her. That she was as happy about the time we had together as I was and yet hurting that it was no longer the same. I chose to feel her joining me in the grieving of what was, and that is no more.

I also chose to feel her joining me in the next phase of my life I was creating without her being physically next to me. I chose to open to her presence and be in her loving embrace each day as I move forward. I knew I had to keep moving forward and I was so grateful for my clarity in being able to do so with her right here with me.

I still miss her more than I can ever describe. What a life we did have together. What an amazing life partner she was. And what an exciting thought it was to imagine still having her presence by my side as I stepped into my next lifetime.

• CHAPTER 8 •

Yes . . . and Now What?

It wasn't supposed to be this way.

I said that at the end of my first marriage. And it eventually led me to Kathy.

I heard myself say that in the days after Kathy's funeral.

It wasn't supposed to be this way . . . and what will this lead me to?

I sat with that question in the quiet of our home after family and friends had gone, unable and unwilling to answer it.

Two months after Kathy's death, I remember looking back on her last days. I had insisted that Kathy get back to the hospital. She was struggling but neither of us even suspected that three days later she would die. Now feeling the reality of her loss, I had a gaping hole in my heart . . . and in my life. Her absence was so present, so big, so full of hurt.

I was aching all over.

I was lost in the loss.

I was in a daze pushing myself.

I wanted to go somewhere and hide and cry and scream and cry and not see or talk to anyone. I wanted Kathy back in my life, in my bed, in my arms and in my presence. I missed her in every way possible.

I hurt in every bone of my body.

As I mentioned previously, Kathy had started a new book in early 2016 that she had titled: *Staying on Top When Your Health Turns Upside Down: How to Navigate the Heroic Journey Back to Vitality and Wholeness.*

The book was to be the story of how Kathy had made her way through her bout with cancer and with that, she was creating a format designed to help others see these major challenges as their heroic journey. She had planned to show how the Hero's Journey storytelling arc could be a valuable framework for "staying on top" while dealing with the trauma of a major health crisis.

In the first few weeks after Kathy died, I reread the book proposal. In doing so, I found the question she had challenged herself with: "Yes . . . and now what?" When I came to this question, two months after her death, it stopped me in my tracks. Wow, here was a classic Kathy Cramer question! And why did I have to find it now? And do I really have to answer it for myself?

Back then, I could not muster the strength or clarity to actually say anything about the "now what?" part of the question.

> *"You came into my life so unexpectedly. You changed my experience of the world, of what it could be like to love another and be loved. You opened a world of grace and beauty and elegance on so many levels and in so many ways. And I know I have to get to the question: so, now what?*
> *I can't answer that question just at this moment.*
> *I have glimpses and I know the answers will begin to come."*

I want to share the passage from the introduction in Kathy's unfinished book that contains this question. It is comforting and inspiring to me to hear her words and through them, sense her own strength and resilience that she worked so hard to help others find in themselves.

> *"After several scans and consultations, I found out that I was facing stage 4 breast cancer that had by that time metastasized to my bones and liver. As my heart sank, I knew full-well that my only (and best) response needed to be "yes and now what?"*
> *But for me, knowing how to respond was a far cry from actually responding in the best way possible.*

I remember feeling waves of sadness descending on me like a dense, dark fog. At a moment's notice, while I was doing something mundane like sitting at the breakfast table eating scrambled eggs, all of a sudden my eyes would well with tears as it dawned on me that I could very well be losing my wonderful life—my husband, my work, my colleagues, friends, my home, my lake house, my puppies, everything might be gone in a flash, without warning, due to the indiscriminate hand of breast cancer that was running wild in my otherwise healthy body. It all felt like a bad dream.

In other moments that came just as frequently as the "fog of sadness" ones did, I felt deeply grateful. Grateful for being given the opportunity to live such a wonderful life. Waves of gratitude would rush over me, bringing with them vivid flashbacks of events and encounters that reminded me just how blessed and fortunate I had been for the past 67 years. From having the life-long support of my mom and dad, to receiving a first-rate education from kindergarten all the way through graduate school, to having the closest, best friends, to marrying the most amazing, loving, generous human being on the planet. I was bowled over by the sheer number of gifts I had received over the course of many years."

All of us who knew Kath are not surprised at these words and how they represented her approach to life in general. It is who she was and how she lives on in each of us.

And so I let her question and her words settle into my heart. I let Kathy touch me in her deep way and it was from that place that I found the strength to begin answering her question for myself.

Yes, Kathy is gone
Yes, I am in shock and deeply, deeply sad
Yes, the life I thought was ahead is no longer
Yes, the pain is beyond any I have ever known
Yes, I can't believe my beloved Kath has left
Yes, it all seems so surreal and totally unbelievable
Yes, I have tremendous support from family, friends and clients
Yes, the questions are endless
Yes, the fear can creep in
Yes, I do know that, in time, all will be okay

AND

Now, I take it a day at a time
Now, I let this grief come and do its work with me
Now, I start to seek clarity for what's next

Now, I begin to define what I want on all dimensions of my life in this rebuilding process
Now, I begin to engage with friends and family in new ways
Now, I create new ways to bring Kathy's work into the world
Now, I explore seriously what work there might be with Mary Beth, Laura H., Karrie and Linda
Now, I dive deep into my own desire to learn more about and explore my OBE work
Now, I decide on my next course (and possible work) at The Monroe Institute (TMI)
Now, I look even more closely at the point of this grief work being in my life now
Now, I create something for the world through KDC/JSD cards and our "fax of life"
Now, I get serious about creating weekend retreats to offer Ready For What's Next
Now, I start hosting small dinners at the Linden house
Now, I continually stay open, in each moment, watching for what else wants to happen

Yes, the sorrow found its way routinely into my life in those days. And along the way, there was truly developing, more space between those times of sadness.

Yes, the sadness called me into its presence, such that I could not turn away. And in that space between, when I paid attention and looked closely, there was joy, happiness and even delight. Here's how I described it at the time:

The call to pay attention seemed more poignant when I realized the significance of the space between, while honoring the space within. And so I forced myself to slow down and give the space between as much care and attention as the times of sadness. I let my focus linger longer in this space between and marinated in the joy, the healing that this allowance of immersion offered.

The smile of a passer-by, a ray of sun catching the rustling leaves, the encouragement of a friend, the shouts of children lost in play.

Each bringing a moment of joy, they are all there and each has its place in the space between.
They were all present for the noticing—once I was open to the world around me.

The moments of joy came and lifted me up, just as the pain of the sadness remained real. Joy and sadness . . . sorrow and delight, each so very far apart, yet held so closely together while being pushed further apart, by the space between. Allowing the moments of delight to be held in reverence then became a must, just as acknowledging the sorrow from loss had to continue.

HOLDING BACK AND LETTING GO

DURING OUR FIRST THREE years together, I was traveling for my work throughout Asia and Europe, roughly half of that time. Kathy and I wrote letters that we would fax back and forth during my time away.

On one of those early trips, I received a poem of amazing depth and filled with a yearning that still calls to me today. Out of Kathy's words came a new view of our relationship. I became her "Moon Man" and she became (literally) the "Sunshine of My Life".

In her poem, Kathy wrote to me: *"How is it that the moon can embrace the sun? How is it that the sun can draw the moon so near it? In those moments of openings are the lifetimes of closeness."*

With that poem, our life together and our love for each other had just been redefined. I knew I was falling in love; I knew the beginnings of what we were describing as our WE.

That simple understanding of our WE then turned into a profound experience. We both discovered what it can be like when two individuals come together so closely that where one stops and the other begins is so blurred as to make it feel all is one.

We became deeply tuned-in to one another. We became acutely aware of a connection that was soul deep. We found our thoughts were inseparable, as became our hearts, our minds, our bodies, our every desire. We began to see what could happen when two people gave-in to falling in love so deeply that the I and the me could not help but turn into our WE.

Kathy wrote then *"Letting go is definitely an act of faith, a sacrifice worth making. Holding on only takes away from the remembering that is possible for me when I honor what has been given and received."*

Our deal had been to be with each other in a way that did not confine each other. To hold the other with that open hand. It was to enable us to be close like never before and still be able to let the other go. When Kathy was in the ICU and I realized, she was not going to make it, I heard myself saying to her that I wanted to back out of our deal, that my open hand wanted to hold on tightly - that I couldn't let her go. Not now, it just wasn't supposed to happen this way.

As friends and family came to Kathy to say goodbye in the ICU that day and I heard all the expressions of how she had touched their lives, my heart opened again to the experience of our unconditional love that we had developed for each other. It enabled me to come back to truly be able to say that "I am holding you with my open hand." Even though I was hurting beyond any hurt I have ever felt, the strength of our "WE" allowed me to hold her close in my heart and let her go at the same time.

I JUST WANT TO TALK

THERE WERE SEVERAL FORMER colleagues of Kathy's who had not been able to make it into town for the actual memorial/celebration service we held the week after she died. About three months later, coinciding with a visit of a couple of those colleagues, our good friends Beth and Paul organized a gathering in their home for many, if not most of those associated with the work of The Cramer Institute past and present. It was the epitome of a Kathy Cramer fan club if there ever was such a thing.

Each one present had been mentored, supported, encouraged, partnered-with and most of all, deeply loved by Kathy. Beth created a beautiful process that allowed each person there to share stories about how Kathy had touched their lives. Those stories touched me deeply and when I was home later that day, I journaled about my experience . . .

Kath, I just want to talk with you . . . just for five minutes . . . well maybe ten.
I have to tell you it was an afternoon that I know you would have wanted to be there . . . yet, of course you were.
I want you to know what it was like to have felt the love in the room . . . and I feel sure you did.

There was so much that was said, that was felt, and that was affirmed.
There was so much more to be said, more to be experienced, and more to be acknowledged.
Yet it was all "just enough" . . . just enough for hearts to be touched, opened, and for some, healed.

The tenderness, the openness and the willingness of all that was shared was moving. The flow of the stories and the connections and the energy it brought was all so up-lifting. The range of hearts being touched, pain being acknowledged and laughter that was found was all so amazing.

We, the benefactors of her attention, of her affection and of her love, got to bear witness to the impact she had and continued to have in our lives.

It was all so clear how she was living on in so many facets of our lives, how she continued to encourage us to reframe and see the world in new ways, how her footprints were embedded in our souls.

I could rest in the love from all those that were gathered, as we found our own ways to offer that love to each other, and I knew that I could reach out to those that were present and keep discovering more of Kathy through our conversations.

TRYING TO LET GO

AT THE CELEBRATION SERVICE, I said I would let her go. Months later, I felt much less able to do so. The enormity of life without her had set in and it was beyond any difficulty I could have imagined.

> *Come to me darlin' and just whisper your Moon Man poem to me in my sleep. Let me feel your closeness and let me know you are okay. I trust one day I will be okay. It is just not today. It is from that place of deep loss that I stop to curl up and sleep until I can find you in my dreams. I love you Kathryn. I miss you like never before. I am trying to let go. I will keep trying . . .*

The following note and poem was written by Melissa Fuoss, a close family friend who was going through her own cancer journey at the same time as Kathy. Melissa and I had also started meeting to explore Kathy's idea of the hero's journey through a crisis of loss. It is through her words and the words of so many others that day at Beth's house, that I realized that we can continue to hold Kathy with us, and that she will always live on in our hearts.

John,
My random act of kindness (our homework assignment) is to send you this email. Is that cheating?

I wish it was Kathy leaving a card for you under your pillow, inside your briefcase, inside your desk drawer. And yet in a way she has.
All that love is not lost. All those words are not forgotten. They are tucked under your pillow, inside your pantry, between the cushions of your couch. They are there whispering, can you hear them?
What do they say? What do they beckon you to do? They have called you off of the shore and into the water.
In some ways, it is much nicer to be on the beach. To just look out at the way the waves rise and fall. To see the way the sun's light slides across the surface. In some ways, it is nicer on the shore.
But losing Kathy has called you into the water, into the truth, into the darkest light. You have been swallowed up by those waves, pulled into the center of the storm, your boat wrecked, your life vest cast away. You've felt the

weight of stones in your pocket, and you've sunk all the way down to the bottom.
But did you notice the way the light bends when you are underneath the waves?
Did you hear that deafening silence?
And what was it that called you back to the surface?
What bubbles of hope lifted your face to the sky?
You are treading water.
But you are in it. You are deep within it.
And it is painful beyond measure.
And it is painful beyond measure.
And it is painful beyond measure.
But it is real,
and beautiful,
and powerful.

And soon, John.
Soon you will be swimming.
When your arms cramp up, and your legs become too tired to kick the waves,
You will float on your back,
The sun on your face,
And you will swim.

But for now, feel the weight of the water. Glance up at the shore stretching out in the horizon.

We are there- waiting for you to whisper the truths of the ocean. Tell us what you see,
Describe each detail, You are in it.
You
Are
In
It.
Tell us what you see.

Out at Sea
by Melissa Fuoss

What a powerful place to be,
Actually breathing within the sea,
No longer sunbathing on the shore,
This
Is
More.
And what are you willing to give?
To feel the weight of what it is to live.
To slay the dragon, to slice the waves
To make the most of the moments that bleed into days.

What a powerful place to be,
Actually dancing in the sea,
No longer just toes touching the sand,

This
Is
The
Plan.
How much longing can you take?
Before your heart will break?

When the sea can give no more,
You
will
find
the shore.

So . . . I don't know where any of that came from . . . just fell out in weird little clusters on the page :) I guess our talk tonight inspired me. Hope you are feeling your power today.[5]

Sending love,
Melissa

STILL HOLDING ON

I WAS FEELING THE loss of Kathy in a big way the Christmas after her death. I did not have her that year, nor would I have her for any other, to celebrate Christmas in the grand and joyous way we knew how to do.

5 Letter and poem by Melissa Fuoss used with her permission.

During those holidays, I had some really good talks with my sister Barbara. I opened up some to my kids Adam and Emily. I had an amazing conversation with my niece Ali at a breakfast meet-up. At the few parties and dinners I attended, I was blessed with friends holding me with compassion, with love and care. I did go be with all the Cramer family for a Christmas eve dinner. I stopped by to see Kathy's cousin Jack and his family for Christmas night. I had dinner with other friends on Monday. Yet the poignancy of being at each event without Kathy, pulled me into a deeper sadness. I simply could not pretend to be in a different state than I was . . . and I really did want to be in a different state.

All of these events reminded me of the emotional drain I was feeling. The tiredness and low energy I felt came from the emotional toll of grief catching up with me. Stopping and doing nothing was very needed. Sleeping in was very needed. Moving into my day slowly was what I had to choose.

I was hurting each day and trying to move through that time in a way that honored Kathy and the season of joy. Yes, there were moments of joy, but it all seemed masked by the hurt and sorrow and sadness. The state that I was in caused me to cancel my plans to be with my family in Oklahoma. That hurt in and of itself to say no to time with them. The state that I was in held me back from being in the constant presence of the Cramer kids. It's not that I didn't want to be with them, but the state that I was in was pulling me into solitude. I felt a great need for quiet and silence to let me hear what my heart was trying to say. It took more resolve than normal to stay away from the "should be" voice that tries to make things better or encourages me to blow past the feelings that are really there. It is an old, old pattern for me to want to be sure others are okay before I am okay.

I wanted to write a Christtmas message that pointed to hope and healing. I wanted to find words that would show others the gift that has been mine in the life I shared with Kathy. I wanted to extend Kathy's legacy of seeing the world through the lens of what's possible. I wanted to be able to stand tall in knowing I am moving forward in a way that honors all of what we had together.

Those were my wants and I did not get any of them . . . at least not right then. Instead, I was compelled to be with the hurt and the sadness, to be gentle with myself and trust those I encountered would understand. Instead, I chose to grieve the loss of having Kathy in my life in physical presence.

This year it is different and that is what I am stepping into this day knowing and feeling. And after that step I will find the next step. And then the next. And with each one I take; I am blessing myself.

My path through grief was only apparent as I looked back to see where I had come from, where the accumulation of steps had brought me. It had to come from my own awareness of what felt right in the moment. There is always so much opportunity to second guess and that is my big watch out. This was a time for me to constantly keep trusting myself and letting that be the best guide for what step is next.

Original artwork by Rosemary Renee' Davis - ©2021

• CHAPTER 9 •

Transformation

If I could find and stay open to possibility, what would that mean?
If I could let Spirit keep touching my heart, how would I transform?
If I truly could speak from my own open heart, what would I have to say?

What was the work I needed to do to step into my life going forward? Was this a question I was making bigger than it needs to be? If I kept coming back to the breath, back to the present, would I look up one day and see that I have created the experience I want on my own?

Or was it a case of continuous intention? Was it that each day I had to be clear with myself about what I wanted that day from this experience? Should I be going back to the Both/And? Maybe there is nothing to do here except be with Both the grieving, And the moving forward. Maybe they will each unfold as they should.

To bring in the 2017 new year, I attended a spiritual-growth focused workshop called the Warrior Monk Retreat.[6] There I experienced a transition within my grieving process. The workshop was held at the Whidbey Institute on Whidbey Island off the coast of Seattle. I entered the retreat wanting to shift intentionally into a new phase for myself. But my grief work had some other ideas and I found myself dancing intensely with my loss, the sadness it brought, and the experience of sharing that grief with the group of assembled seekers.

The start of the Warrior Monk retreat left me feeling tentative about where I really was with myself at that moment. It felt like I was holding-off my grief. I could feel it right below the surface and I knew how it opened me when I let it show up authentically. I realized then I wanted to simply let it go and let it come out whenever it comes out, rather than trying to hold myself together. I wanted to let go to find the emptying, so that the emptiness would become available. Being there, I realized I had the opportunity to create the experience that I wanted, if I would just let myself do it.

During the retreat, that group of strangers (along with my sister Barb) held me in their unconditional love, in a way that was truly transformative for me. As transformative as had been the unconditional love I experienced with Kathy. The time we had together

6 https://warriormonk.org/

was monumental and significant and real and filled with love and beyond my wildest dreams and so unexpected. I discovered a stirring, deep within, that said I must rise from this moment into something I could never have imagined otherwise. I could not simply have lost Kathy for me to go sit silently in the corner. I couldn't have given up my soul mate if there were not something really important ahead.

There was an offer, a view, a possibility that wanted to be heard.

Now what will I do with this one wild and precious life?

I saw what Kathy had done with hers. I experienced what we had done with ours. I began to imagine what I could possibly do on my own. During the time Kathy was with us, her presence for all of us was a continuous call into possibility. For me in the presence of that group, I began to sense the new possibilities for me.

THE PORTAL OR THE CRADLE?

THE MAIN MEETING ROOM for the retreat featured one wall that was all windows looking out onto the beautiful grounds of the Institute. The first day there I noticed this large stone sculpture, in my picture above and was drawn to it right away. Called "The Portal", it is a stone sculpture by artist Lloyd Whannell, on the property of The Whidbey Institute. He lives near the Institute on Whidbey Island, WA. This piece was donated and moved to the Institute grounds by a member in honor of his wife who died at their home. The member was sure he saw his wife's spirit pass through "the portal" as it sat in the backyard of their home the moment of her passing.

I know the sculpture was titled "The Portal" and yet, the moment I saw it at the retreat, given the state of grieving I found myself in, it looked more like a cradle.

I sensed how the smooth curved interior surface was wanting to hold me in the moment, to surround me and comfort me and let me feel all that I am feeling, to honor all that was present.

This portal now cradle, was a gift I could only find right then in that particular place. This portal now cradle, could only have been seen by my stepping into this unknown experience. In stepping in, in letting go, I opened, I felt, I released. I chose to grieve.

As I let my loss and longing simmer, then boil, then go cool, then explode, then go quiet, I began to feel the cradle shift its shape. As I let all of this emotion flow through me, the cradle gently nudged me out of its loving embrace. It caused me to stand before it and see it in its intended place--as a portal.

And as I looked at, into and through the portal, one thing became very clear. My true cradle at that retreat was actually the circle of strangers who had quickly become loving friends. It was in this circle that I was being held and supported and encouraged. It was in this circle that there was a love so clear and apparent that it brought a whole new set of tears.

Near the end of the retreat, I was able to tell those who had been with me that week: I want you to know that in being part of a cradle, that you have formed to hold me, one that you never asked to join, you also have created the portal through which I can now emerge. I can now confidently step through this portal and do so even though I know nothing about life on the other side.

Their compassion created that cradle, and it was a very transformative gift. The portal they offered was the invitation I had been longing for to create my next version of life.

NOT AGAIN . . . YES AGAIN

WELL, I THOUGHT MY week of quiet at the retreat would have let me settle-in and be ready for a strong start back at home. I thought my focus on the transformative retreat take-aways would enable some peace.

But back at home, the experience of loss enveloped me once again and I could not think my way out of it. There was no doubt that what came next would be a dance, a dance between what was the cradle and the place I was trying to reach on the other side of that portal.

I see the life I have had on one side.
Will I leave her behind if I step through?

I don't know the life I can have on the other side.
Will I ever find myself if I step through?

"Come with me through this portal."

I hear the voice so clearly.

At first, I imagine it is her voice calling me to join her.

Then, I know it is my voice, inviting her spirit to be with me as I explore the longing that will be my next version of life.

I told myself that it wasn't supposed to be this way anymore, that somehow the pain should be starting to go away. But it was back, the pain was very present. Not again, I told myself.

And yet . . . I knew my work in the moment was to turn this "not-again" into my own "yes-again."

Yes, again I shall rejoice in the time that was ours.
Yes, again each time I turn and see your smile, let it draw one from me.
Yes, again each time the hurt becomes so poignant, let it take me to the joy that was ours.

Transforming the not-again to the yes-again helped to move the energy. Yes-again enabled my focus to shift to all things amazing about my life with Kathy. Yes-again invited me to honor and celebrate and revel in all we had as our WE. Holding our WE close, remembering how that understanding took us to so many new "yes-agains" was the way of my transformation.

Kathy's love was the force moving me forward, providing the guidance for taking that next step, holding me ready for what will present itself next. It was and still is a love so clear and present that I can feel her holding my heart in her open hands. Love builds strength. Strength brings new possibilities.

THE WAY FORWARD

Fear surrounds my heart to join me on my way forward.
Fear tells me I can't be sure of what I need to do next.
Fear whispers that I may be moving too quickly.
Fear holds me in its grip saying that moving forward means leaving Kathy behind.

Sadness comes to remind me of how moving forward can feel.
Sadness helps me see what I have with me as I move forward.
Sadness holds my loss ever present and helps stabilize me as I move.
Sadness defines the depth of unconditional love that our WE was holding.

Joy can creep in between the fear and sadness and show me light.
Joy touches my open heart and offers its healing.

Joy calls me to bring all that WE have had and move forward with delight.
Joy helps me know that all that has been is still with me, as she will be.

Anger boils knowing it should not be this way.
Anger rises to protest the unfairness of it all.
Anger spews its bitterness at having to rebuild my life.
Anger brings the unanswerable cloud of why me, why now, why her.

Love stands by as the fear, sadness, joy and anger dance.
Love holds a place of knowing that all is as it should be.
Love offers the new world of possibilities.
Love reminds me that nothing has been lost, that Kathy is present, here and now.

In the moments after the retreat, the presence of Kathy's love gently embraced all that was stirring within me. In those moments, my love for her filled me to overflowing. I was filled with the knowing that our love holds true, that there is nothing to fear, but there is sadness to honor, joy to embrace, anger to release, and love to allow into a broken, yet open heart.

This was when the way forward became a part of the knowing, knowing that what was unfolding was good and true, pure and delightful, clear and sure. One moment, one step, one more step. In the calm of this knowing was the clarity that I would be bringing forward with me what was, and that it will always be a part of what is.

IN THIS MOMENT

In this moment, I feel the heart inside that is so broken open.
I feel the gaping hole that remains from losing the love of my life.
I feel the raw pain and hurt that is still so present.

In this moment, I am aware that this broken heart is a heart opened in a new way.
I am aware that my sense of possibility has been heightened through this newly opened heart.
I am aware that possibility and openness bring newness for hope and transformation.

In this moment, I cry as I look at each picture I see of Kathy.
I cry for what I thought would be that now is never to be.
I cry for the aloneness I feel without her here in this room.

In this moment, I know I am not alone in spirit.
I know I have her here within, around and beside me.
I know that all the love we shared is held within this broken, open and whole heart.

In this moment, I seek the wisdom to make sense of all that is swirling within.
I seek to let the broken-openness serve to guide me to what's next.
I seek to honor all that was and hold it for what it is now and let it become what it will for going forward.

In this moment I trust that brokenness, awareness, openness will lead to a new sense of knowing.
I trust that in staying present clarity will emerge in a gentle grace-filled way.
I trust that my willingness to courageously speak from my own open heart will let me hear the words needed at just the right time.

In this moment, my open hands are holding Kathy so closely.
My open hands are bringing her love for me and mine for her, together to fill every cell of my heart.
My open hands reach out to offer this love anew for myself and to each that I encounter in the world today.

In this moment, I find solace in my belief that this process I am swirling in, is just where I am supposed to be.
I find grace in allowing myself to give voice to all of this that is within.
I find acceptance that is so elusive and fragile, beginning to hold me in gentle new ways.

In this moment, I choose to honor this acceptance.
I choose to hold Kathy even closer than ever before.
And I choose to let all of this show me, in the moment, the next step to take . . . and then the next.
In this moment, I am here, I am present, I AM.

HEART HEALING ON ROBERT'S MOUNTAIN

In March of 2017 I attended a meditation workshop on exploring consciousness at The Monroe Institute (TMI)[7], a retreat center in the Blue Ridge mountains of Virginia. Keep in mind, this was three months after the New Year's retreat at Whidbey Island. TMI was founded by Robert Monroe to research human consciousness, after he started having his own out of body experiences. I had the privilege to meet Bob before he died, when I went to the Institute for the first time to explore and try to better understand the out of body experiences, I had been having back in Lifetime #2.

7 https://www.monroeinstitute.org

Paula was one of our facilitators for the workshop that had started on a Saturday. During the introduction session, I had only vaguely referred to my loss and mentioned Kathy's name only once. The next day on Sunday evening, Paula had us find a partner to begin an exercise on exploring our intuition and internal guidance. I connected with Diane, an energy worker who had come from Puerto Rico, and as we were leaving the room, Mark who was there from Australia, asked if he could join us. Of course, we said yes.

The three of us sat down in one of the library rooms upstairs in the Nancy Penn Conference Center at TMI. Diane and I sat down on the couch and Mark pulled up a chair he had found in the hallway. We were the only group of three for this exercise, which had followed a full day of meditation exercises.

My turn came in the intuition exercise we had been assigned. I was to think of a question about something of importance going on in my life at this time. My job was to get quiet and just think the question to myself, not saying anything out loud. My partners' jobs were to tune-in to themselves and then to me energetically, listen to the guidance that came to them and offer what they received as answers.

I was sitting there with my eyes closed letting the question float out each time I repeated it to myself. On about the third time of "sending out my question," I heard Mark gasp and all of the sudden say, "John, Kathy is here, she is here in the room with us right now! I can feel her energy wrapping around us, I can feel her love right here with us. I feel the strength of her love so clearly right here. Do you feel it?"

He then went on . . . "John, I see Kathy's energy. She is right here but she is stretched upward toward a light. It looks like she is holding on here and trying to get there. She is saying she can't go there, not yet. She has been here all along wanting to know that you are okay. She wants to know if you are okay and won't leave you until she knows you will be alright."

Mark was sobbing and in tears and just kept saying over and over, "I feel so much love from her. It is right here, so much love." By this time, I too was in tears and just sitting there trembling. I was witnessing an encounter, feeling the energy, yet not "hearing Kathy speak", rather, just knowing that Mark was having a direct experience of and with her. I started crying uncontrollably.

Mark then asked me, "John what is your question?" I said it out loud for the first time: "What do I need to let go of at this time to help me move forward in my life?" He almost shouted back at me, "John, Kathy wants to know that you will be okay. She has been here not able to let go of you and she has felt you wanting to keep her here as well." I said something like, "oh no, I never meant to keep her from moving on, I never meant to hold her back. I miss her so much and I know I will be okay. I know I have to let her go. I know she has to let me go too. "Kath, I will be okay, let me go so you can move to your light. I will let you go as well. I had no way of knowing I was holding you back."

Mark was still sobbing and said, "She is surrounding us with love, I can feel it like she is actually here touching me. It is that strong. It is amazing. She says she loves you so much." Through my tears, I said how much I love her as well, how much I care about her being able to do what she needs to do next. Mark said, "She is leaving now, she is letting go and moving away, up toward that light."

I was sitting there in stunned silence, just crying, feeling overwhelmed with what had happened, not able to believe what we had all experienced. I was shaking and feeling drained and very unsure of myself physically. So, we just sat there, the three of us, and just held that sacred space together.

Mark left momentarily to tell the rest of the group we would not be coming back for a bit. Diane then asked if I would like her to do some energy work to help me get clear and integrate what had just transpired. So, I sat on the floor with my eyes closed, while she then helped move my energy and the energy in the room into a very calm, positive and healing place. She was able to help me settle into what had happened by enabling me to feel quietness return inside. My breathing slowed, my body relaxed, my tears would not stop.

How was it that Mark just happened to join me and Diane at that last minute? How was it that he was so tuned-in to spirit that he was able to experience and translate Kathy's presence? How was it that Diane just happened to do energy work that was then able to help me integrate the experience in a really good way?

The letting go process that Kathy and I exchanged that Sunday was a huge gift for me. As I did more to integrate that gift and settle-in to the continuing meditation experiences over the next couple of days, a lightness within me became apparent. A sense of newness was present, yet my letting go was still incomplete. And that all led me into my own direct "heart-connection" experience of Kathy, which happened that following Thursday in the afternoon meditation session.

Healing, lightness, excitement, overwhelming love, unbelievable closeness and a soul connection all became part of me after this next experience. They were all part of what pulled me forward into my own "what's next." It was comforting beyond belief to know that the same was happening with Kathy. I captured the Thursday experience in the following notes from my journal.

She Held My Heart

The quiet in my meditation was all around me, completely holding me.
My breathing slowed to allow a deep in-and-out movement that created a calm, focused rhythm.
My mind accepted the quiet, began to follow the breath and in doing so, it brought along my fragile heart.

My intention was to give in to the dance I have still been doing between holding on and letting go, between wanting the life that was and finding the life that is to be. I have been afraid to fully let go and yet now is the time. I want to release the fears that have really been playing the music of my dance.

My intention was to bring wholeness to my heart still being split between wanting her here and living with her gone. The fear and anger, behind knowing she has left the physical plane forever, holds me from being able to connect in spirit. I want to find the courage to let go, so we both can truly start our next phase.

My intention was to find a way to both honor the incredible love we share and get a glimpse of how to carry that love forward in all I do. I want to clear the negative energy I am holding around losing her and open myself to all the love that is within our relationship, no matter what the form is going forward.

I noticed my breath, my thoughts fell quiet as my mind accepted the stillness, which let my heart begin to open. All of a sudden, we were in our old neighborhood where we loved to go on our walk-talks. I heard my heart begin to speak . . . .

"Kath remember our first dinner when I could not answer if it was to discuss the work project or if it was a date? I remember the twinkle in your eye as you asked that question. Do you remember the twinkle in my eyes as you let my hand take yours for our first dance to the music I brought to Innsbrook?"

"Remember each of the many other times we were able to dance with each other? The weddings, the New Year's parties, the moments alone in our living room. It was one of those moments that was captured in our 10th wedding anniversary painting. Remember our delight as that statement of our love was unveiled?"

"Kath there are so many of these moments, there are so many ways our love was shared. You brought a love to my life I never

knew could be possible. You opened my world into so many new dimensions and in doing so, filled my heart so completely."

"If you were really here, I would want to look into your eyes once more to assure you that my life is forever changed because of your love. My life is so large because of what you brought to me. My heart is forever blessed because you chose to love me in the way that you do."

In that moment, as we were having our walk-talk in the quiet of my meditation, I noticed we had stopped at #27, one of our favorite homes on the block. In that moment, as I spoke of how blessed I am because of her love, I felt this most wonderful, incredible blanket of energy surrounding me. And in that moment, I felt her literally hold my heart in her hands. I felt her love flowing through her open hands into my broken heart, offering it healing and peace and a grace that was unimaginable.

As I let that love flow through my entire being, I reached up to take her hand and the moment I felt her touch, we were on a beach. It was dusk, the sun was setting, the waves were rolling onto the sand. I remember looking over and seeing her face so clearly. Her bright blue eyes were twinkling like I had never seen before. The warmth of her smile was radiating love around and through me.

I looked over at her, grinning ear-to-ear and said let's run! Your hip is okay and my knees are good on the sand, so let's run. We took a few quick steps, began to jog, looked at each other and then broke into a full run. We started laughing and kept running and as we ran faster, I looked up and saw that the sun was about to touch the water at the horizon. I turned to Kathy and I said, "run Kathy, run and touch the light, now is the time". Our eyes met, my heart was pounding, and I heard myself say to her "good-bye Kath, good-bye for now, go, go to your light." I let her hand go and I watched as she flew into the sunset.

She held my heart in her hands. I hold her love in that same heart. Each time now that I go back to her touch, I feel the healing in my heart. I know the broken heart is now giving way to a wholeheartedness I have never known possible. And it is with that whole heart that I can step into my next phase of loving this life like never before. And now I can truly say, "I can't wait to see what happens next!"

CHAPTER 10

The Threshold Crossing

There is a lightness, a sense of freedom and empowerment.
There is clarity, release and excitement.
And there is a new openness for what will next show up.

The clarity and release are telling me I have crossed a new threshold.
I have stepped from the place where pain and loss have defined me.
I have stepped from the place where grieving has consumed me.

The lightness and openness are showing me I have crossed a new threshold.
I am stepping into a place where I feel excitement for what's next.
I am stepping into a place where I know I can choose to engage with life in a new way.

I know that my grief will continue to present itself as I go forward.

I know I may be stopped in my tracks at times I get reminded of losing Kathy.

And I know the power from simply being present to those moments will enable my movement through them.

That sense of confidence and knowing bring the feeling of empowerment.

The feeling of freedom then comes from being able to truly be okay with not knowing what will happen next yet being able to welcome it.

This is a different place . . . it is a new place . . . and I find myself here because of all my work, with all of the support that has happened over this last year.

I have crossed a new threshold.

I am in a new place.

It is an unknown place . . . and I am choosing to step in and be present and available for what wants to happen next.

My heart, that has been broken open with pain and loss, is now experiencing a wholehearted joy that is enabling a very sweet transformation.

One long year after Kathy's death, I was feeling just how different things were. I looked back at all the steps it had taken to get me that far. I could sense the importance of taking each deliberate step. And after that step I found the next step. And then the next. And with each one I took, I blessed myself.

Inside, her voice told me: "Embrace the sadness, the loss and the effort it is taking to move forward. Let it all be okay and let it all do its work with you. Hold yourself open and available for what shows up. Be gentle along this path and know it is leading you to something beyond that will be life-giving."

I was finding ways to open myself even more deeply to this loss, to invite all the wisdom in me to show itself and provide guidance for going forward in my new life. There was a lot to draw on. There was a huge love story to tell about what we had between us and what now I could find within me.

I had so much to be thankful for, so much joy to step into, an amazing array of just how many ways two people can create a beautiful life together. I had all of that still with me. I had all of Kathy still with me.

I now knew Kathy was okay and I believed she knew I would be okay. I felt I was on my way to being okay. I was able to say to her in my heart, *"May we continue with this dance, with our dance, until we can be together in whatever way is next. May my patience with the process and trust in the not-knowing be strong and true."*

And for sure, the truth back then on so many days was that my way forward was so clouded that I could have easily just stopped and given in to the despair that I so desperately wanted to go away. Every day, I danced with the acceptance and the disbelief... and I made no promises for tomorrow. All I could promise myself was that I would show up open, hopeful, and with intention, as each day presented itself. It was with that intention that I held the place of possibility for myself going forward. My heart that had been broken open with pain and loss was beginning to experience a wholehearted joy that was enabling a very sweet transformation. And it was because I chose to let my broken heart give way to a wholeheartedness, I had never known possible. I let it show me, in the moment, the next step to take . . . and then the next.

There is a part of me now that can look back at that year after Kathy died and realize that in one sense, I had come full circle. For it was that condition I set at the beginning that seemed to have still been in play after Kathy's leaving: "If this relationship has served you in all the ways possible, while I still may want to hold on to you, I do so with an open hand. And that means you can leave anytime to find what's next for you". Now at my own threshold, I was also clear that Kathy was off on her "what's next" adventure!

TRULY LETTING GO WITH AN OPEN HAND

Kathryn, you suddenly appeared at my office doorway and then as we started dating, I told you I would hold you with an open hand. It was my way of saying, I am committed and if this relationship is not working, you are free to move on. During the next three years of my travel and many letters exchanged, we found a love develop that was so unexpected.

We started our time of marrying and as we were creating our life together, I held you with an open hand. Yet while my open hand held you close, your open hand held me, as we kept falling more deeply in love. Together, we realized we were holding each other in an unconditional love with our open hands, as our way of saying be just who you are.*

Your mighty cause emerged and as your writing reached its pinnacle, I held you with an open hand. It was a time of bringing to the world the power of your ABT mindset and helping others see new possibilities. We found our own new possibilities, as we forged a time of working together every day.

You were diagnosed with cancer and as you navigated treatment, I held you so very close, with an open hand. You found your own open hand, when you asked the question: "Yes and now what?", as you navigated your own way forward, until the days in July, that turned out to be your last. It was then in the ICU when I tried to back-out of our open-hand deal, as I realized you were about to leave and never come back.

We gathered at Villa's Chapel and as I stood before all those whose lives you've touched, I did my best to let you go with an open hand. It was the love you brought to me, it was the love you brought to everyone present, that helped us know you would be in our hearts forever. And still it has been a time of continuously finding how hard it is to truly let go.

It's already been a year, a year filled with grieving that has been intense. As I sense your presence Kath just beyond the portal, I feel my heart overflowing with love. It is a love I never believed could be possible, and it causes me to reach out now with my beckoning hand, to draw our love even deeper into my very open heart.

**We always saw our marriage as a verb, something that continued to evolve, and so we always referred to it as "our marrying."

Lifetime #3.5 Perspectives

MY EXPERIENCE OF LOVE

I EXPERIENCED SO MUCH love from so many that supported me in the year after Kathy died. Being held by that love was life-giving, especially in my very lowest moments.

I know there was so much self-love in trusting my process of grieving, sometimes out loud, many times in the silence of my home. I was able to pay attention to myself and what I needed in ways that could have been judged as selfish and yet in reality, I was giving myself the gift of singular attention when I needed it the most.

Throughout all this time, I have reconnected again and again with the unconditional love that was the experience of my time with Kathy. It has continued to be present, regardless of the emotional state I find myself in at any moment. By allowing the flow of sadness or anger or fear or whatever the expression of grief took on, always brought me back to that place of love. It is a place that will never go away and that I will be consciously bringing into my life going forward.

MY EVOLUTION IN CONSCIOUSNESS

Awareness of feelings was the headline banner for my evolution in consciousness in Lifetime #3.5. The whole range of emotions was a part of that year of grief work. Sometimes they were as clear as a bell, other times one was hidden by another. My choice to be conscious about my grieving allowed each emotion to have its time and do its work.

I now know so clearly that when I am able to be present to my deepest feelings, there is an internal, soul-level movement that becomes possible. And that movement brings new awareness which leads to healing, if I can just stay with it by staying present.

My own understanding of my consciousness has taken on new levels from my awareness now of the depth that a hurting soul can touch. I had never felt the kind of pain in the grief work that has transpired in this brief Lifetime #3.5. Yet I see how it has brought such new insights into what was possible to learn because of my willingness to experience the pain.

I am now clear that if I let my feelings flow and stay with the emotion that is present, that it will all work itself out in a good way. I know this now in the depths of my heart. It is a heart growing in understanding, growing in awareness and sensing that in finding wholeness it is possible to live every day in the level of consciousness that is experienced as unconditional love.

A MOMENT TO REFLECT . . . ON LIFETIME #3.5

EVEN WITH ALL THE other losses in my life, the grief that came with losing Kathy was more painful than any that had come before. The work that was required to process that pain and honor that grief seemed never ending at times. I can see now the ways I was able to find strength to move through that year after Kathy died and I have such gratitude for that time.

I know what my family and my extended family did to support me. I know what my friends, my work colleagues, our Cramer Institute clients and so many others did to help me through that time. How can I ever express the depth of my appreciation?

As soon as I ask that question, the answer comes clearly. My appreciation is best expressed by going forward and creating an amazing new life, a new life that reflects the depth of love that surrounds me and holds me, that comes from each and all of those in my life. A new life that is lived with joy, happiness, love and care for all that are a part of it. A new life that is consciously created, that becomes a greater expression of self-love and that will become a way to extend the experience of unconditional love that was brought to me through Kathy. My desire, my focus, my mission became to create a world of unconditional love by living fully and courageously from my own open heart. And now I am fully exploring and living that mission in Lifetime #4.

Original heartwork by Jaxon Wesley Davis - ©2021

Lifetime #4: Finding My Way to Unconditional Self-Love

IT WAS IN MONTH thirteen after Kathy died that I found myself able to say, "I am ready to start a new life for myself."

That was the beginning of my Lifetime #4.

There was a lot that happened for me, to me and through me in that previous year. It was as if I stepped through a portal in time the day I heard myself say I might be ready to actually create a new life for myself. It was a huge moment.

This and the closing chapters of this book attempt to share yet another completely unexpected experience with unconditional love, my journey to truly unconditionally loving myself. It is best summarized as: I had it, I lost it, I started searching for it again . . . and then, I found it had been within me all along.

It has brought me to consider a very hard question and the challenge in it:

What is possible if unconditional love is consciously present in my life every day?

MY 4TH LIFE MANIFESTO

I create a world of unconditional love, by living fully and courageously from my own open heart.

I choose being present and authentic in all my relationships.

I choose intentional personal growth to discover new levels and layers within myself.

I choose enthusiasm as the experience of my work and creating transformation as the impact.

I choose personal vitality through a lifestyle of daily exercise, enjoying what I eat and maintaining a strong, healthy heart.

I choose having enough financially for me and my family and enough for helping others.

I choose making a difference by giving back in intentional ways.

I choose being fully present for how I use my discretionary time whether what is showing up each day is intended or spontaneous.

MY 4TH LIFE FOCUS OF THOUGHTS

BY STAYING PRESENT, IN each moment, I experience:

- Joy through my happiness,
- Health through my well-being,
- Abundance through my generosity, and
- Love through my unconditional acceptance of self and others

Original artwork by Rosemary Renee' Davis - ©2021

CHAPTER 11

Consciously Creating My 4th Life

"As you give thought to your future—your future that may be 10 years; your future that may be 5 years; or your future that is 60 days away—you literally begin preparing for it. And then, as you move into those pre-paved moments, and as that future becomes your present, you fine-tune it by saying, This, is what I now want. And all of those thoughts that you have put forth about your future, right down to this moment when you are now intending what action you want to take, will all fit together to bring you precisely that which you now want to live."[8]

---

8 From *The Art of Allowing* workshop series by Abraham-Hicks, ©Jerry & Esther Hicks, AbrahamHicks.com , (830) 755-2299.

https://www.abraham-hicks.com

From my Lifetime #3.5, a time of doing the hard work around grieving, I found the clarity and confidence for moving forward. Warren, my therapist, helped me see that the path of grief work and the thread of grieving will run through each element of change I began working with in this new life. Almost four years since the beginning of this fourth lifetime, I have touched the depth of loss several times.

Yes, the grief is still present . . .

. . . and it does not define me.

Grief is still a part of me. Every aspect of my new life is touched in some way by my loss, including my relationships. The loss does not define me or these elements, yet it is a common denominator with a voice in each area.

When I found that clear, strong energy and excitement about moving forward and creating a new life, the daily hold of grieving somehow lifted. I found myself knowing I was ready to move forward. It was a very liberating realization... and a very scary one at the same time. In a way, the day-by-day process of working through my grief had become a very familiar place; my grief offered a kind of comfort, one that would have been easy to hold on to for a while longer. However, the holding on would also have resulted in a holding back and I came to find myself wanting to honor the feeling of excitement about stepping into my next lifetime.

My work in this lifetime is to let that voice of grief speak when it must and to give it space for expression. I believe that continuing to acknowledge this grief when it appears, allowing it to be with me when needed and surrendering to it, is enabling my next steps to continue to emerge in a powerful and clear way. I believe my "what's next" is benefiting from allowing the grief to flow as it must and do its work as it will.

When I found that I had come to the place of really being able to move forward with living a life not defined by grief, I realized I had come to a very unique place. I saw that I had an opportunity to create literally any kind of life that I wanted. I was in such a very fortunate position to be able to say, I truly can create any life that I want. It is a very sacred responsibility.

I decided that I would get very intentional and begin a process of consciously creating my new 4th life. What choices were important to consider for each facet of my life? What would my life look like if I very deliberately brought those choices together into something I had never experienced before?

This caused me to step even more clearly onto the path of unconditionally loving myself.

I wanted to know what it would be like to be so intentional and so deliberate as to imagine what I want and then get out of my way to let it happen, and then to revel in and savor the results. I knew it would lead me to be even more deliberate about "what's next."

My process for beginning to define what I did want next for my life became a very big effort. One that I worked with over several weeks. I literally started with a large blank page.... about the size of my dining room table. I adapted for myself the work I do with clients in a coaching process I call, *"Ready For What's Next."* In that process we have numerous discussions to articulate a "life mission," one that would bring meaning and purpose. I then ask clients to describe what they would define as a life well-lived going forward. We look at seven dimensions, including relationships, spiritual development, work life/career, physical well-being, financial well-being, giving back to the community and use of discretionary time.

Through my own discernment, I set an intention that described how I chose to create a focus in each dimension. I then gave myself time to specifically detail what I wanted to see be a part of each of those focus areas.

It turned into quite the colorful and detailed "mind map" and was a very exhilarating experience. Each dimension has quite a bit of detail that made sense at that time. It continues to be a work in process, however, it does a really good job of defining what my new life, well-lived, could look like. Following is a summary of my own mission and seven intentions that have become my "4th Life Manifesto."

MY 4TH LIFE MANIFESTO

I BEGAN CREATING THIS 4th Life from a place of awareness and a level of consciousness not present in my previous three lives. Above all, I found myself clear about choosing to make this lifetime intentional and significant.

When I first heard myself say I want to make this new life "significant", it raised all kinds of doubts and possibilities at the same time. It still does. But instead of shying away from it, I have been encouraging myself to let that statement stand so that all that follows will be with the intention of finding what "significant" means for me in this moment. The first piece of that is what I am now calling my mission for this new life.

I create a world of unconditional love, by living fully and courageously from my own open heart.

I will speak to exactly what I mean by "living fully and courageously" in the chapters ahead.

Truly, my challenge with this 4th Life has been to surrender any attachment to a specific outcome, and as I will describe in some detail later, to let go of "figuring it out" and to always stay present. I developed a way to help me be aware of and more purposefully, think about my thinking. Awareness of my thinking has become a critical practice, which I call My Focus of Thoughts. It is my way of setting my highest level of daily intentions and of opening myself to this new beginning—even though I have no idea where it is headed!

MY FOCUS OF THOUGHTS

By staying present, in each moment, I experience:

- Joy through my happiness,
- Health through my well-being,
- Abundance through my generosity, and
- Love through my unconditional acceptance of self and others

This is also a reminder for me to keep learning and growing. Which leads me to the seven intentions for my 4th Life . . .

I choose being present and authentic in all my relationships.

I want to develop new levels of depth in my relationships with my family and friends. As I grew more comfortable with the idea of a new intimate relationship, I also wanted to step into the world of dating.

I choose intentional personal growth to discover new levels and layers within myself.

My intention for my spiritual journey was to continue building my personal spiritual practices, deepening my self-awareness, intuition, and my experience of my higher self and spirit guides. I want to gain a deeper understanding of non-physical reality, study energy work and the practice of energetically sending love and healing to others and to myself.

I choose enthusiasm as the experience of my work and creating transformation as the impact.

My intention for my work is to create a self-aware world by coaching and facilitating transformational experiences in which participants learn more about themselves. And I will do this through their having an experience of being fully seen and heard. To do this work, I want to continue to work on finding the courage to speak from my open-heart and moving past my own reluctance to share more deeply. I trust myself so my clients know they can trust me--and in doing so, they can then trust themselves.

I choose personal vitality through a lifestyle of daily exercise, enjoying what I eat and maintaining a strong, healthy heart.

I will practice physical well-being through all of the activities I enjoy - biking and elliptical work, walking and hiking, snow skiing with my son Adam and scuba diving with my daughter Emily. I will continue with proactive health care through the functional (integrative) medicine practice I have found and consciously choosing a diet that supports my health, weight and well-being goals.

I choose having enough financially for me and my family and enough for helping others.

I am focusing on balancing my income from working, with income drawn from savings and retirement resources. I am creating a deliberate approach for helping fund grandkid college educations and helping others in need.

I choose making a difference by giving back in intentional ways

The ways I am giving back include volunteering with the organizations that I hold dear, like College Bound, Barat Academy, COCA the Center of Creative Arts, and the ManKind Project.

I choose being fully present for how I use my discretionary time whether what is showing- up each day is intended or spontaneous.

Now it is my time to play! I am honoring the activities that I enjoy like travel and live music. I am re-igniting my love for photography. I am developing new reading pathways and thoughtfully re-engaging with daily news and politics. Through all of my experiences, I continue to ask, "What's really going on here?", as yet one more way to keep learning.

I get to completely make up what I want my life to look like going forward. It's quite the realization. I am not bound by any real constraints. Now is my time to create the new and for sure, my time to play.

This deliberate creation is a very intentional act. It comes from knowing that "thinking about my thinking" is actually an act of creation itself. I have seen what can happen when I set my intention in a clear way, hold that focus and let go of the outcome. This is an extension of that experience and that practice applied to every other facet of my life.

It is a big step to be so willing to create a new life for just myself. My challenge is to keep finding the depth of self-love that makes it possible to keep my excitement and focus on what it is I want my next phase to become.

It feels like a lot of work in one sense and there is a discipline involved as well. It is also coming from a deep inner knowing AND it is an act of faith, all at the same time.

• CHAPTER 12 •

Being Alone : Being in Relationship

I NOW KNOW I do not *need* a primary relationship to live a happy and fulfilled life. It has been long enough now that I know I can live on my own, alone, and be quite okay. I also know I *want* a primary relationship and the clear desire behind that, is coming from wanting to both share and create a new life together with a significant other.

I will love again like I have loved before. I will love even beyond what I have ever known. And I will be open and ready to be loved as never before. That is my open heart and my whole heart, healed, speaking loudly and clearly.

I actually started a new relationship about fifteen months into my 4th Life. It was a surprise at how easy it seemed to get started, there was a chemistry that allowed us to really connect. There was a playfulness that was compelling and a desire to learn more about who we could be together. There were also really strong existing lives we each had in place that, as it turned out, did not really want to be altered. I ended it almost three years later, after several stops and restarts along the way. It was hard to end—there had been a love growing despite the struggles—yet it was not enough to hold me through the hard parts.

Through work with my therapist Warren, I was able to get objective feedback on what more I needed to do to create a healthy relationship. Through my subsequent processing, I have worked hard to pull out those lessons and changes that seem important going forward. In my men's group I have been challenged even more directly to be honest about how I show up in my relationships. (The men's group is part of an organization I have been a part of for over 18 years called the ManKind Project, discussed in more detail later in the chapter.)

WITH ALL OF THIS support aimed at creating better relationships, I learned that:

- To always be clear about what is going on for me, what I am feeling and why. (And yet to be able to say it in clear language, so it could be heard.)

- I had to re-learn that what I want is as important as what the other wants. (A lesson I was sure I had integrated from my failed first marriage – in my 2nd Life.)
- I don't have to accept less than what I want. (Especially in a relationship.)
- There are times when I really must bring a hard, masculine energy to bear. (This hurt to have to face the fact that it was always easy for me to default to a softer, more accommodating energy, driven by my desire to be liked.)
- In a related manner, it is critical to match direct and hard responses with a like energy. (Again, my ego screams out at admitting I needed to learn such things.)
- Judgment and criticism challenges me to stay in my open-heart space. (I believe the criticism was also a challenge for me to look even deeper at "my stuff".)
- To live from my own open heart, regardless of where the other might be. (While maintaining compassion, empathy and acceptance of the other.)
- And maybe most importantly, that my love can flow unconditionally for self and the other,

regardless of what is and is not coming to me. (A learning that will require frequent reminders.)

It was several months, after leaving that relationship that my aloneness one Sunday morning became quite overwhelming. I sat on the couch sipping a cup of tea with my puppy dog Sophie close by and my emotions began to pour out of me. There was a big rush of sadness that hit me, followed by a gripping fear, then came an anger that wanted to rage. That anger led me to guilt and, most surprisingly, a rare sense of shame that finally swept through me. It all happened in a few minutes; each emotion was as distinct as the next. I found myself cycling back through one and then another, when finally, I said STOP!

I took a breath and slowed myself down to pay closer attention to what was really happening here. The aloneness had triggered a wanting and desire to be with another, to have a beloved in my life again . . . and yet, there I sat, all alone.

That was the sadness, as I acknowledged . . . I was sitting there all alone.

The fear was that I may never have a relationship with a beloved again.

My anger was because Kathy had actually died and left me alone.

The guilt was because I should have been able to make one of those new dating relationships work.

And then that surprise of shame: Who am I, that I can't figure out all this relationship stuff?

BARBARA: NO DANCING IN CIRCLES FOR YOU!

THE NEXT SUNDAY, AS happens almost every Sunday, I had a call with my sister, Barb. I told her what had happened, and she helped me think through the experience even more clearly. By the time our call ended, I was actually feeling joy. Joy from the depth of our connection and conversation. Joy from the parade of emotions I was able to let myself experience, process and better understand. And joy that, deep down, I know that another person will appear in my life – or me in hers – and I will find myself creating an entirely new life with someone new. That is a surprise worth waiting for, even if it means more Sunday mornings on the couch alone.

As my sister reminded me during our call: "Letting yourself really experience your parade of feelings as you fully processed through aloneness was really important." She was right, I now realize it was a way of demonstrating unconditional love for myself by not turning away from those feelings. Letting each and all of those emotions be expressed in that moment, hearing what each had to say to me and being open to learning more about myself from those messages was, in fact a very compassionate way of loving myself.

It helped that Barbara had been willing to slow down with me and not only hear what I was saying but also get a sense of the feelings that were present that day. She ended the conversation with such a loving reminder: "You are, my dear brother, a fearless observer and participant of that parade, even if it includes the painful discoveries. Sitting with your feelings, especially the tough ones, is an act of unconditional love for yourself. That tenet of unconditional self-love has always been within you, and Kathy gave space and recognition to it even before you knew that component of your relationship."

My 3rd Life was all about the Dance with Kathy. Now, as Barb pointed out, the reciprocity of that dance with my partner stands in stark contrast to my current life, dancing alone, dancing in the dark, dancing in circles, and sitting out dances entirely.

My new path is filled with present moments, where I must continue to choose to show up for myself unconditionally, Barb told me. And that skill is gaining more and more momentum for my unconditional love of self to find expressions. "No dancing in circles for you!" she ended.

How can I ever adequately express the love I have for my little sis?

This relationship with my sister shatters the aloneness that I so often feel. She is there for me at any moment and for any reason.

Our relationship has grown exponentially since we attended the Warrior Monk retreat. That shared workshop participation became the foundation of an ongoing experience of growth and learning together. We chose to attend that retreat together, as it was focused on those seeking to create a transition of some kind in their lives. I was transitioning to a life after Kathy and my sister's was finding a new life after divorce. One of the early lessons I learned, as we continued our post-retreat explorations and conversations, was that her loss of a partner (through a failed marriage) was just as significant as my loss of a partner (through death). She helped me see how similar our struggles were and how parallel our paths were. I came to see how the impact of any significant loss was very similar, regardless of what brought on the loss.

My empathy and compassion have taken huge leaps forward, as Barb and I have continued our Sunday conversations together. These are times of respite, joys and sorrows shared and unconditional love experienced.

THE UNIQUE GIFTS OF FRIENDSHIP

IT TAKES A LOT of self-love to stand in this excitement that I feel around my 4th Life. Each time I talk with someone about where I now find myself, I get very emotional. That tells me how important it is to speak about this and at the same time savor the experience of loving myself unconditionally in this moment.

I have made it this far into my Lifetime #4 with the help of an amazing set of relationships, some that have just shown up and others that I have created. I have nurtured each of them and all of them have given (and are giving) me unique gifts. As I take stock of the family and friends, the men and women who have been and are with me, I am overwhelmed by the depth of care and love that we share.

I find it very interesting–and most compelling–that I have developed a number of deep and meaningful relationships with a cohort of women who are now an integral part of my life. They don't really know they are a cohort as such, but they do know how much they each mean to me. In these relationships, I have found yet another form of unconditional love.

Several of these relationships only came into my life after Kathy died. Each allows me to be my most real self and open my heart without reservation. They have each offered guidance and love and have been open to my version of the same. They help me learn and grow each time we talk – and we have maintained a routine and rhythm to our talks. These are very conscious conversations from which I am getting so much value. Without having tried to do so, I am having an experience of unconditional love. At least that is my experience of them and with them.

I know they are each in my life for a reason. I also know they are each a unique gift for which I am deeply grateful. Ours are conversations that literally "bring me alive" and bring me to know what a life is void of judgment and lacking in fear. It allows me to be open and vulnerable. That is a huge gift.

KAY: MAKE YOURSELF AVAILABLE AND THE UNIVERSE WILL RESPOND

I MET MY COLLEAGUE Kay over 20 years ago, at a work-related conference. She was doing leadership consulting work at that time, as well as finishing one of her leadership books for publication. I hired her to work with me on defining and establishing the culture within a new organization I was creating, part of the joint venture in China for the electronics company I was working for at the time.

We reconnected in the year after Kathy died. Since then, we have been in an ongoing conversation where we talk at least every three to four weeks. These calls have become a time of openness. We initially let ourselves talk about experiences of grieving, my loss of Kathy and her loss of the relationship with her ex-husband, along with a myriad of other topics. The conversations on loss led us into a recognition of how each loss had brought us into so many new places that would never have been found otherwise. Now these conversations allow us to explore way beyond the topic of loss.

In one of our conversations on new relationships, Kay posed a set of very challenging questions:

> What if I showed-up in the relationship as I want to have it?
> How have I created what I don't like in the primary relationship I was struggling in?
> Do I have the courage to step through my fear and find the courage to make the hard decision to end the relationship?

I have found Kay never settles for the easy questions!

A little over a year into my 4th Life, as I prepared for some time alone at a self-created retreat in reflection, Kay posed another set of her infamous questions.

Somehow, she is always able to find just the right questions at just the right time:

> Where am I in my 4th Life so far and what do I now want for my focus?
> What will I find if I hold the wonder of the child and actually expect to find something wonderful?

That last question is one that I love to go back to time and time again.

Kay challenges me to allow vulnerability to be okay. She has helped me see that I must allow myself those personal and emotional heart-risks. That is what will open my heart. It may be that living with an open heart could be the safest way to live. I know I do not want my heart shutdown. I have seen how painful that can be. Her questions keep pushing me to dig deeper and risk more sharing and I am very grateful for both.

It had been two years since Kathy died and I had decided it was time to do another level of "clearing my past". The new home that Kathy and I had moved into was furnished with what we had accumulated together over twenty years. Most of the furniture had been moved from our previous home. We had been in the new house only three weeks when Kathy had to go into the hospital . . . and never came back. So, even though we hadn't really had the chance to make it "our" home, it was still furnished with all of "our" pieces and the daily reminder just kept pulling me back into the past.

In one of our conversations, I was telling Kay about my intention to refurnish my home and the doubts I was having around even doing something like that. I think I was trying to convince myself it was an unnecessary project and that I could just keep living with it.

Then the questions came, as usual.

You're talking about replacing physical objects, but what is it you are really wanting/needing to let go? Look at your resistance from a spiritual perspective and ask, what is it about finding my new home (and life) that I am resisting?

What if your job at this moment is simply to surrender to your sense of guidance and let happen what wants to happen? Take time and answer the bigger question: who am I and what is home for me now?"

From that conversation, I went on to spend a bunch of money and have a lot fun in finding new stuff for my living spaces.

The importance to me of our conversations became so clear when Kay described a process of significant transformation that she had been experiencing. She had moved through some intense physical challenges that had allowed her, in essence, to create a spiritual rebirth for herself. As I listened to her tell her amazing story for over an hour, I came away with a critical understanding for myself: It was a true gift for me to bear witness to her story of transformation. Hearing her joy, and feeling her relief and excitement was exhilarating. Being present as she sought the best way to use her new lens into the world was a very special honor.

A very special piece of wisdom that keeps coming up in our conversation is around approaching something in an "effortless" manner, rather than getting caught in "efforting". It comes from the belief that miracles happen when we create an approach that is effortless, easy and enjoyable. I just love that as an ongoing challenge and litmus test for a new "effort". This, for me, is yet another example of how Kay's wisdom keeps finding its way into our conversations.

Another conversation with Kay evolved into what might happen if I could totally let go of wanting to control things. What would it be like to set an intention, then let go of any attachment to an outcome, to give up on control, to surrender. This line of thinking brought us to the metaphor of the labyrinth. Well, it was actually an extension of a real-life process Kay had used in some of her group coaching work: Walking the labyrinth as an act of surrender. The intention for the process is to end up in the center. The process is to step on a stone, stop and just be there. The challenge is to be open to being guided at each step. Ask when and where to step next, trust your guidance, and take that step. This requires letting go of control, maintaining your intention and a willingness to trust that voice within or your intuition or whatever you experience as guidance.

The conversation turned to the opportunity that can be found if I were to live my life as if it is a labyrinth. Play with it, enjoy, be in joy. Be with it and see what the next step is and be open to taking it. Make myself available and the Universe will respond. Be totally present, listen and then notice the synchronicities that emerge.

Conversations with Kay always amaze me, always stimulate, always challenge my thinking, and are always over before I know it. I feel supported by her encouragement, cared for with her questions, and never judged because of my answers. It's like she is entering each conversation from a place of unconditional love. I know I am.

ALEXANDRA: BECKON EACH OTHER WITH OPEN HANDS

I MET ARTIST ALEXANDRA at the Warrior Monk Retreat that my sister and I attended. During one of the break-out sessions we were paired together for a series of discussion questions. When we got to the question on what our heart was calling us to do next, Alexandra began describing her "legacy sculpture" work. She had started working with families, communities, and individuals that had experienced loss and creating three-dimensional memorial sculptures. She described it as a creative process and a healing process as well. Given the loss that I was still processing at that time, her work caught my attention, and we began a conversation that still continues today.

Given where I was emotionally at the retreat, I was very interested in what her process might offer me, how it might help me move through the grieving that was still very persistent for me. When I returned home from the retreat, Alexandra and I began the legacy process she had described to me during our time together. She started with a discovery phase in which I described the relationship I had with Kathy. That took me into a reflective phase, where she asked me deeper questions about my life experience with Kathy. These were gentle, yet probing questions meant to give me a chance to fully express all that Kath had meant to me. Alexandra provided a very safe space with her very careful listening heart for me to explore many levels of feelings about my loss.

I found it very cathartic to open-up to someone who had not known either of us and attempt to explain the depth of our relationship. It did indeed become apparent after several weeks that I was experiencing a new level of comfort and healing in my time of grieving. Through these conversations, Alexandra began to move into the creative phase and started to produce ideas that were coming to her from our talks. I don't know how she did it and what I do know is how right it felt once she hit on the right image to represent the relationship.

The significance of my relationship with Kathy being built on "holding each other with an open hand", emerged as the theme of the sculpture. My open hand actually letting go of Kathy's hand in that moment of her transition became a compelling image that Alexandra based her sculpture on.

As she neared the completion of the production phase, the question of what to title her piece of art came up. As I saw the image become clearer through her sculpting process, I was moved into a surprising place, given where I thought I had been in my grieving process. While I know I had been describing my open hand letting go of Kathy's, as I watched that piece of Danby marble take shape, all I could feel was my hand reaching out, yearning to hold hers one more time. That yearning is what led to the piece becoming "The Beckoning Hand".[9] I simply let that phase of grieving be what defined my experience of Alexandra's work of art.

---

9 https://moroscofinearts.com

She brought the sculpture to my home; we created a wonderful one-year commemorative gathering and unveiled the artwork at that time. It was a heart-warming time with family and friends and truly did serve to help me transition into this Lifetime #4.

Alexandra and I still talk at least once a month. She has become a trusted friend and confidant. We share many conversations as fellow spiritual seekers. We talk about relationships and life in general. I've helped her think about her own career steps. She helps me think about all kinds of next steps. We hold each other with our own open, loving hands in each conversation. I continue to grow each time we talk.

ANITRA: THINK ABOUT YOUR THINKING

About a year after Kathy died, a call came to the office from Anitra, a young woman involved in organizational development and leadership work in Denver. Anitra had started working with Kathy before she died. I had not met her during that time. When Anitra called, it was to ask if we could start a conversation about continuing the work started with Kathy in some way.

It became clear to me very quickly that Anitra is a kindred spirit, as well as a talented coach, trainer, workshop leader, mediator and mom. She is a natural at Asset-Based Thinking® (ABT)[10], which is why she and Kathy had been working together. Anitra shares a passion with me around the Laws of Attraction and that quickly gave us more of a jump-start into our conversations.

I remember early on in those conversations, we found ourselves in the territory of the importance of "thinking about our thinking" and how critical mindset management is to achieve our desired results. We had a very robust discussion on ABT that literally brought us alive because we both saw the promise of what being deliberate and conscious about our (ABT) mindset can offer. There are many more examples of how similar in approach we found our organizational and coaching work.

Anitra has become a great sounding board, an active thinking partner and a friend who can be very encouraging when faced with a challenging flashback of when we were working with Kathy. However, we also found that there is real clarity and power behind our thinking to have our work-related (and any other) discussions in between runs on the Colorado ski slopes!

JILL: LIVE YOUR LIFE IN JOY

Yet one more significant relationship that has emerged for me is in knowing university professor Jill,

10 www.assetbasedthinking.com

who is affectionately known to all her friends and campus colleagues, as the Dean of Joy. This is a truly earned title, based on how Jill lives her life every day. Granted it does not come with an endowed chair, however, it does speak to the impact she has in everyone's lives that cross her path. Jill is a bundle of joy and as a positive psychologist, she practices what she preaches.

We met through our mutual interest in leadership development and over the years, while the work-related focus continues, we have actually become very close friends and confidants. We partnered in delivering several workshops together and always seem to find a way to stop in at her favorite ice cream store. Over many coffee times, we have found a connection that certainly enables me to learn more about myself each time we talk.

Jill has a way of challenging my thinking and some of my actions (especially concerning relationships) that is nonjudgmental and full of compassion. And it's not just with me, that is who she is in the world. She has often encouraged me to be more open in expressing my feelings and shown how it is possible to hold both joy and sadness simultaneously.

JOHANA: DON'T HOLD BACK–HOLD SPACE

About a year after Kathy's death I started working with a shaman healer, Johana[11], which for me has become very soul-level spiritual work. In our sessions, she offers guidance, challenges my thinking, does some very in-depth energy work, all of which has enabled me to find new levels of spiritual growth.

Of the many things Johana has helped me with, one was working through a particularly dark, yet key experience I needed for my own growth. It was during the time of the initial relationship that was developing after I had started dating. In trying to sort through the ups and especially the downs that seemed to be coming more frequent for me, I had lost my feeling of being centered and grounded. I had lost the lightness that is so familiar when I know I'm in my place of unconditional love.

Johana challenged me to remember that "I know" I have that place of unconditional love still within me. I needed to get myself clear about the trigger that caused my negative reaction that was now present. What was it that I did not want, that was happening in the relationship which was really a reflection of what was in myself? She told me to remember what I believe about unconditional love being who I am deep inside and how

---

11 https://www.johanahealing.com

that helps me hold my own space for self-compassion. From there I could find my way back to myself, from my ego-self to my Higher Self. From there I would reconnect with my unconditional love for myself and be able to better accept the negative stuff that was coming up for me.

However, it was also necessary to consider if this was about shifting into a "conditional love" for myself or within the relationship. Was I reacting negatively because things weren't going exactly as I thought they should be? Was I not leaving room for my partner to have her reactions to things and letting that be okay? Did I give up the experience of unconditional love because of something I was wanting or wishing that wasn't there, or because of something I believe different than what was the reality in the relationship? In other words, was I only able to be in the place of unconditional love as long as things were going the way I thought they should? The answers to these questions really made me realize I was back into conditional love. And so, this became a moment to look at what I was most scared of - which was losing yet another relationship. But it was also a chance to grow and learn more about myself if I could see the original negative feelings as an opportunity.

Through it all, Johana's encouragement was to keep imagining my light shining, even in the darkest part of the cave, and it will lead me back to myself. I hold the light within, and I will be able to find myself, even if there appears no way out of the cave.

As I worked through this phase, Johana helped me see a very important practice and perhaps principle to keep in my awareness: in times like these my job is not to hold back, but rather to hold space for myself (or another) and trust in my ability to navigate through the trouble.

Expressed in a slightly different way, using another metaphor, she encouraged me to stay in the flow of the stream and when an emotional hook catches me and pulls me onto the shore, acknowledge what has happened and look around at where I am. Then jump back into the flow and keep moving with the stream. Keep working to get good at this, while acknowledging my growth in being much better at doing this now.

Don't hold back—hold space.

BARB B.: FIND A CREATIVE WAY TO BREAK THE RULES.

Kathy's best friend since kindergarten was Barb B. Although she has been in my life now for twenty-five years, she is here in a new way since Kathy died. Barb has been a source of strength, encouragement and support in every way possible. She has offered consolation and just as often has sought it.

Barb and I will have catch-up calls that inevitably go deep into exploring our emotional states. I experience her as always so very open about what is stirring for her and the level of hurt or pain that is present. I love to hear her recall a story of Kathy's support or wisdom that came at just the right time for her. I can't help but laugh at the many escapades they created while "raising each other as kids". This as she explains, means that while growing up, both sets of parents were either too busy or their parenting was too dysfunctional to have been the type of support they each wanted at home–so Barb and Kathy created it for each other.

The famous line that defined them both was that, if there was a rule in place at their all-girls Catholic school, it was their (self-appointed) job to find a creative way to break it. Barb assures me that no rule was left untouched by the two of them. These stories are always heart-warming, funny and most often poignant. They speak to the depth of the friendship that was shared between Kathy and Barb and they represent the significance our friendship has developed since Kathy died.

What I have come to value most in this friendship with Barb are the times we get to spend together when visiting each other. Those conversations always become both soul-searching and soul-revealing discussions. Through our common avenue of grief, I have found a way of sharing that has brought healing and love into my life in such a heart-felt way. I find myself so grateful for the depth this relationship has found and for the grace that comes with each of our conversations.

MANKIND PROJECT: UNCONDITIONAL LOVE IS SOMETIMES TOUGH LOVE.

THEN THERE ARE THE men in my life . . .

I have been involved with a men's organization now for over eighteen years called the ManKind Project. MKP (for short), as the website states, is "a men's community for the 21st century. MKP[12] is a nonprofit training and education organization with three decades of proven success hosting life-changing experiential personal development programs for men. The organization supports peer-facilitated men's groups that guide men in leading lives of integrity, authenticity and service. All of this is aimed at developing men who are emotionally mature, authentically powerful, compassionate and purpose-driven, who will help heal some of society's deepest wounds."

---

12 https://mankindproject.org

For the last two decades, I have been meeting with my group of ten men, twice a month. They have become my most significant source of support in every facet of my life possible. At the same time, they are the ones who will challenge me to look deeper at "my stuff", in order to become the best person I can be. They have offered me a safe place to be open and vulnerable, because I know I am held continuously in nonjudgmental love, in an unconditional - and very tough - love. This continues to be an amazing gift in my life.

On a normal day, these men are there for support, to challenge, to help find a way for healing or growth . . . all through a pure, non-judgmental, raw and honest unconditional love. And that is not an overstatement by any stretch. Taken as-is, the "normal day" approach is a gift beyond measure. On the days when grief set in and I had no way of seeing my way through, they provided nothing short of a life-saving presence. And that is no overstatement either.

To be held literally, as well as figuratively, emotionally and intellectually by a group of men who represent nothing less than the epitome of integrity and authenticity, is truly the gift of a lifetime. It has been for me anyway, on so many occasions. I trust these men with my life, and I know that I can come into their presence, open my heart and soul knowing there is safety, love and compassion. This is and has been a big deal for me . . . I have grown immensely through this work and through my association with these men. Never would I have imagined being loved unconditionally by a group of men . . . until I met my MKP brothers.

BILL: THE GIFT OF UNRELENTING, DAILY SUPPORT

I MET BILL, MY best friend from high school, over 50 years ago and we have managed to stay connected and a part of each other's life since then. There have been quiet times in the connecting and there have been active times. We have lived in the same city or close a couple of different times over those years, but most of it has been apart.

Bill is the guy who you know loves life the minute you come into his presence. I always get recharged and inspired each time I am with him or even when we talk by phone. He is open, frank, probing, forever curious and always clear about his love and friendship. He is so wildly passionate about living his life and it is really quite contagious. He will ask the tough questions without blinking an eye. He will dive deeper for more details or meaning without hesitation. And he will be there in an instant if there is any hint of need.

Since Kathy died, I have received a text from Bill every day. Sometimes it's a simple hello, other times it's a rant about some political ploy. He is the only person in my life who has been that consistent in checking-in and staying connected on a daily basis. I've tried to tell him on occasion how grateful I am for his unrelenting support, love and concern . . . and I know my words fall short of just how thankful I am for his friendship.

WARREN: FOCUS-IN ON YOUR TRUTH

EARLIER, I MENTIONED MY therapist, Warren. I sought-out Warren for counseling to do some deeper dives into my grief work (one of his specialties), as well as seek his help to sort through the impact that my on-going bouts with grief were having on my attempts to build a new primary relationship (the one I mentioned that did not work out).

I've already discussed some of the lessons learned from my work with Warren and would add that he has become a source of on-going wisdom for me. He can cut through my BS, my attempts to "dodge the question" or my run-around answers and guide me to focus-in on my truth, no matter how hard it might be to face. There is something so life-giving to be able to touch those truths and then explore the "so-what" for my life.

One of the big questions that came out of our work and my continued reflection on the lessons-learned from that failed, initial 4th Life relationship, has turned into a very compelling challenge. In that initial relationship, I felt judged and criticized a lot. In the conversations with these other significant women and men in my life I've just discussed, I hardly ever feel judged or criticized. That makes it easy to be open and vulnerable. That enables getting to know each other and myself at new depths.

This leads me to the question – and to the challenge – wondering if both can be true at the same time: can I find a way to be open and vulnerable (staying in my own open heart), while being judged and criticized by another? If so, wouldn't that be a good thing?

Of course, in developing an intimate relationship, why would I want to stay in the presence of negative judgment and criticism? Would it be an ultimate test of unconditional love or simply a denial of what might simply be two incompatible individuals? Warren is always pointing me back to what it is my heart is telling me, regardless of the question. I am challenged to focus-in on my truth. In this case, I finally came to admit it was just not the right type of relationship for me at that time. I feel very blessed to have him as a confidant and a trusted counselor.

I realize now I haven't shared a dream with Warren that I am interpreting as a message about a coming relationship. I know that there will be someone to come along, and it will be an amazing surprise when it does. I have an excitement brewing, knowing that even such a surprise is coming. In the dream I had, I was drawn to and clearly attracted to this young woman who I was helping in some way. I knew I was intending to get close as I helped her. Then another woman showed-up to offer a suggestion and some guidance. As the young woman left to find her way with the guidance, the other turned to me and said, "each time I see you I fall in love with you." "Please just hold me now." I wrapped her in my arms, held her close, felt the tears of joy and realized this was a surprise I could never have imagined. I just collapsed in the realization that there really is someone coming into my life that will fit with what I want to do and someone I want to be with and that together we will create the next version of a life together.

However, I am not going to get ahead of myself. I know the process will flow all in a good way, all in the right time. I have made it this far into my Lifetime #4 with the help of an amazing set of relationships, that have both just shown-up and that I have created. I have nurtured each of them and they have nurtured me in ways far beyond these few examples I have shared. I feel it is important to have the significance of these relationships clear and understood. For it is through all of them that I know I will continue to grow personally and learn more about adding depth to my new life. Each in their own way bring an unconditional love into my life every day. And there are many other friends that do the same, that I have not mentioned here.

As Kathy often said, we can't do this alone – it is in relationship that we get to see who we really are. So, while I may be alone at the moment, I am never without a significant relationship. And as a result, I get to keep building an amazing 4th Lifetime.

• CHAPTER 13 •

My Open-Heart Journey

I HAVE BEEN DISCOVERING what it means to live in the moment, to be in the experience of unconditional love, especially for myself, and as a result, to see how life unfolds in an amazing way every day. Part of that understanding comes from looking at two questions: What does it mean to live from an open heart? What does living passionately each day look like for me?

That's when I realized it is essential to consciously stay in the present moment if I am to live with an open heart. Hold each moment in joy—that's when my heart opens. To sustain that open-heart place, I have found how important it is to keep letting go of outcomes and to be willing to surrender and trust that everything in this moment is okay.

Conversely, I have also come to realize that I quickly close my heart and get into my head, when I am always trying to figure out everything. And, believe me, I am constantly trying to figure out everything. It often attaches me to doubt and worry that completely leave behind the unconditional love of myself. So, I keep challenging myself to come back to simply being present . . . right here . . . right now.

These realizations came after a series of "ah-ha" moments, that began months before, while attending an Energy Medicine workshop at The Monroe Institute. The weeklong workshop was training to become certified in the practice of Reiki energy work. Reiki (a Japanese term) is the Universal Life Force energy that is all around us and that flows within each of us. The workshop included several daily meditation sessions, healing and energy flow technique instruction and actual experiential "hands-on" learning.

A fellow participant, whom I'll call Becky, had the experience of what I heard her describe as seeing into the heart of a "beautiful man", while practicing a Reiki healing session. That man was me. I heard her repeatedly say: "you are such a beautiful man; you are such a beautiful man." This experience came during one of our practice sessions while I was on the Reiki table and it seemed like to me, she was literally experiencing or perhaps sensing my heart chakra energy.

Becky later described to me how the experience was one of "wonder and awe" to realize a man could have such an open heart. I believe it was somehow a moment of seeing who I am at a soul level. We decided in subsequent conversations, it was an experience where we had been brought together to open each other's hearts to an even higher vibration and a higher level of consciousness.

That conclusion came after I decided to use this occurrence as a chance to challenge myself and look at a couple of questions that came up for me as a result:

- What is Becky seeing in me that I could now be ready to see in myself?
- How is this a chance for me to understand more of who I really am, at a soul level?

The next day, during a massage session, two more questions were added when the therapist (who is also an experienced energy-work practitioner) asked, as she was working with me during that time:

- What is it that my heart is holding-back right now?
- What is it that my heart is now wanting to tell the world?

I had not talked to her about the experience that I had the day before, nor I had shared any personal details about my life, as a part of the session. The fact that she brought me these questions really caught my attention, in light of the questions I formulated after the experience with Becky in the Reiki session.

During that week, as another challenge for myself, I was also working with the question of creating a direct connection and awareness of my spiritual guides. I eventually came to the point that week of simply letting go of that desire and just trusting. That trusting and letting go then brought the awareness of their presence with me, through a clear sense of knowing, that left me feeling deeply grateful. I can see it now, as both an experience of self-love through trusting myself and one of unconditional love from the presence of my guides. I have gone on to expand that trust by letting that sense of "knowing" emerge, in those quiet times of meditation in particular, when a new awareness comes to light for me.

I then found myself looking at the nagging question of what's blocking me from living from my heart, on a more continuous basis? I began to wonder if it was around insecurity on what's next for my work. Or perhaps my uncertainty around my relationship at that time, and the judgment and negativity that was a part of it. There was also another round of grieving that showed-up, which also had a negative impact on that relationship.

In that relationship, I became aware of my holding back, due to feeling judged and often getting a negative reaction to something I said or did. That raised my awareness around conditional self-love (or maybe more accurately, lack of unconditional self-love), while loving another in a relationship. In contrast, I also was in ongoing conversations with Kay and Anitra, my close work colleagues, where I was always able to feel open and vulnerable by choice and free to say what was on my mind, knowing with them there would be no judgments or criticism.

Those conversations were times when I felt most alive and passionate and willing to freely express myself. I knew I was being accepted in an unconditional way for just being myself. There were similar experiences in my ongoing conversations with my sister Barb and with my two other friends, Jill and Alexandra. These conversations were all times that were showing me how to stay in my open heart. I was able to hold a place of heart-felt joy and unconditional love, for each of them and from them, as well. The struggle within the other relationship also helped illustrate how self-doubt and accepting less-than for myself was bringing me to a place that closed off my heart space.

OPENING (AGAIN) TO GRIEF AND LETTING IT GO

As I briefly mentioned in the discussion of my therapist Warren in the previous chapter, I had an unexpected encounter with my grief over losing Kathy. It happened on a Friday during a morning workout. Before going to the gym, I had been reading a new book, called *LeaderSHOP Volume 2*[13], by Dr. Rodger Dean Duncan that featured an interview with Kathy. As I was reading the interview about her leadership work, I heard her voice through those words that I remembered so well. Once at the gym, out of nowhere, the sadness of missing her just rolled out. It hit me so hard in the moment that I had to stop my exercise routine. It had been a long time since an episode with grief had happened that way and it became necessary for me to sit down and just feel the sadness. Like I had done many times before, I sat there in tears and just let the grief flow through me.

Later that day, I was able to find a deeper sense of letting go, than I think I had known before. By that I mean, after I had processed through the sadness in this case, I came to a greater sense of peace with where I am right now. I knew I wasn't holding on to the past and my old relationship with Kathy. I was still feeling the significant sense of freedom to keep moving forward and the joy that brought in. I really let myself revel in

13 https://www.duncanworldwide.com/

the progress of understanding where I am now. I was able to see how this could have an ongoing impact for me, in the sense of propelling me onward, with happiness in my heart. I knew (again) I was not defining myself through my loss any longer. That felt like a huge dose of loving myself in a new way.

MY HEAD AND HEART DANCE

It was during my men's group one evening, that I heard myself talking through my challenge to live from and with an open heart. As I often do, I was trying to think my way through the question and rationally figure it out. And when I get into my head like that, I can always count on one of the men challenging me to look at my dilemma in a different way. On that particular night, that challenge turned into the two questions I mentioned in the introduction to this chapter:

- What does it mean to live from an open heart?
- What does living passionately each day look like for me?

I left that meeting knowing these were important questions for me in this journey of understanding and experiencing unconditional love, as I live my life on a daily basis.

The answers to these questions began to become apparent to me after experiencing two weekends that truly were lived in joy and flow. One weekend was with my daughter and some friends and the second was on a ManKind Project (MKP) weekend training.

The weekend experience with my daughter was supposed to include a baseball game that Saturday evening, but she ended up not being able to attend. In the morning at my MKP staff meeting I made a couple of random offers and one of my ManKind friends said he could go. I remembered going into the meeting saying to myself, if it is supposed to happen, someone will be available to attend the game. And so it was.

After the meeting I drove to my daughter's place to meet her for lunch. That lunchtime was filled with nonstop conversation that also went into deep places of sharing. I knew I was being completely present because of the ease with which the talk kept progressing. It was effortless and enjoyable; it was light and heavy at times; it was filled with laughter. I also knew how present I had been because time just disappeared. I went on to the baseball game and that experience of an easy free-flowing conversation continued.

When I was back at home late that night, I reflected on how each part of my day had just led to the next part without any effort. I saw how it all had been weaving together as if I had planned it all out well ahead of time. I think what made it so special was because I had simply let go of my need to have things be a certain way and surrendered to just trusting everything would work out for the best.

The following weekend, I was on staff at an MKP experiential training weekend for about twenty-five new men just joining the organization. I maintained a quiet confidence as I handled all the assignments I had agreed to perform and also whatever I saw needed to be done. I knew I was adding value in each simple act of service. I had no need for attention during the weekend, yet I was making clear, heart-felt connections the entire time I was there.

I found myself smiling a lot and I was intentionally channeling love-energy into the circles of men and into each man I spoke with throughout the weekend. I was holding that higher frequency vibration of love, embodying unconditional love and the higher consciousness that is my "ice cream" place (I'll explain this in the next section). Plus, I even had the traditional midnight ice cream treat (with chocolate sauce) on our last night together!

I noticed that men were coming to me throughout the weekend, seeking counsel, advice or suggestions. I noticed that there were a number of meals I was called on to offer a blessing – and I am not what MKP calls a declared "Elder" (one who would normally be expected to bring those blessings). I took all of that as a reflection of the love-energy I was intentionally bringing to each situation and to each encounter. I also accepted it as a reflection of my own sense of self-worth, all stemming from that quiet confidence and clear sense of self-love.

That MKP weekend was a direct experience of joy and flow. It held many examples for me of what can happen when I let myself love my life and love myself and when I hold the vibration of both for a continuous period of time. I was in a very centered place the entire time I was there, which allowed me to just be myself. The deep abiding love that I held for myself that weekend came through in all my encounters.

As I look back at those experiences the two really important points I touched on earlier, came into clarity for me:

- Be in the present moment
  - My heart opens when I can be present
  - The present is where I find it easiest to feel joy
  - Being focused in the moment makes it possible for me to most easily let go of outcomes and be willing to surrender and trust that everything is as it should be right here right now

  - Being fully present allows me to tap into that trust of myself completely and in doing so I am loving myself unconditionally
- Stop trying to always figure out everything
  - This keeps me in my head
  - This attaches me to doubt and worry
  - This can take me to feelings of fear and being anxious
  - It is in my head when doubt and fear get amplified, and I fall totally away from being able to love myself

As I reflected on the effortless and joyful experiences during these two weekends, these two points were what I saw as the "secret sauce" for the joy and flow that was so evident. I realized I had been able to just truly be present and be aware of my being present. It was powerful and so very energizing. Even as I write this, I feel that surge of energy within me, reminding me of the truth I was learning for myself.

My time at The Monroe Institute and with my MKP men's group began to really bring clarity for me on the dance that I can do so often between my head and heart. I saw my learning and understanding come together to include:

- Being present really opens my heart.
- Trying to figure-it-out activates my head.
- Staying present lets my heart lead my head to what's next.
- Setting an intention lets my head create direction and my heart dictate action.
- Letting go of the outcome allows my heart to guide me to the next step.
- Surrendering to this flow and trusting myself leads to just the right place that will align with my stated intention.

These learnings represent for me what it means to live from an open heart and how I can help myself touch the passion that is present when I find that place. And there were even better places than this, as I was soon to discover.

FINDING MY ICE CREAM PLACE

In one of my sessions with Johana, the shaman healer, she was helping me explore my journey into unconditional love. At one point in the conversation, I finally came to understand the importance of finding the feeling that is present in my experience of unconditional love. Johana got me there by asking a very simple question: "What is your favorite food?"

My response immediately was, "ice cream!" I felt the spontaneous smile appear on my face and the energy jump from my body when I responded, and she told me to capture the feelings I was having right then. Those feelings were delight, joy, light-heartedness, and fun. I was actually able to find that physical feeling, that level of vibration within my body, and it is what I can associate with the experience of unconditional love. It has become a really clear anchor for me, as well as a practice to keep actually sourcing those feelings for myself.

It really is a good-feeling place–try it for yourself. Think of something, someone you were with or a time when you felt joy, delight, fun and a sense of lightness. Remember the circumstances or the experience itself and savor that experience for just a few moments. Pay attention to what happens in your body when you do that. Doesn't it start to really feel energizing?

Back to that moment with Johana . . . it was a very familiar energy; in that it is what I have felt when I talk to others about my experience of unconditional love. It was so revealing what that vibrational, energetic feeling-place associated with loving ice cream so much represents for me. It is the feeling I get when I am always open and loving.

That work with Johana opened a new understanding for me and I used it to create a challenge for myself. The challenge has become finding my "ice cream place" and holding it vibrationally and energetically on a continuous basis. If I hold myself in that vibrational frequency of unconditional love, then I know all will be okay. Everything is as it should be. In that open-heart space, things, people, relationships will show-up, drawn to that vibration because they too are at that frequency. The challenge has become to hold this frequency of vibration for myself, no matter what else is happening to me or around me. I know I can find unconditional love when I don't have to have certain conditions to feel good. In other words when I don't attach conditions to my experience of love or offering another my love, that is what unconditional love is about for me.

Here's a big question that I have been trying to answer: If my well-being is defined by maintaining a high vibration for myself and a vibrancy in life, is that dependent on something outside of me or is it totally dependent on my staying in alignment and grounded within myself? My answer is the latter. If I can stay true to who I am (aligned with my Higher Self) and not let my ego take over, I can find my way to a place of unconditional love more easily.

I am learning not to give in to what I can't control (even though my ego tries to convince me I am in control). Instead, I am trying to surrender to staying in my own power, my own alignment with my Higher Self. I am focusing on what I can control without having the need for anyone else having to line-up with me. To quote from the book of fellow Warrior Monk participant, Eva Live: "Be so in love with my life, that I will live so in love with my life. When I love myself, I can love you."[14] Eva's words help me remember that I must unconditionally love myself first before I can hope to bring that love into the world on a continuous basis.

This heart-opening phase of my journey has been so significant. It has represented such an explosive phase of growth and understanding. It has brought me to know that everything is quite okay and all that is coming into my life offers gifts and blessings I could never have anticipated.

AND I am completely aware of having set my intentions in this very direction. I think about my mission of creating a world of unconditional love and much of what I have just discussed represents my own life being filled with it—especially the huge dose of self-love that has become possible because of this work.

---

14 *Being and Belonging: A Memoir in Poetry* Used with permission from author Eva Live. https://evaliveawake.com

Original artwork by Rosemary Renee' Davis - ©2021

• CHAPTER 14 •

Holding My Life with An Open Hand

IT HAS NOW BEEN over four years since Kathy passed. It seems like yesterday; the time has flown by and I have experienced so much that has helped me move forward.

I have a new lifetime that continues to emerge, and it is offering so many opportunities I would have never thought possible. I can now see that I have been given the chance of a lifetime to create this completely new life. There was a time when I could not have imagined it would be possible for me to say that. And I sit here excited, exhilarated and really open to what's next, it feels very empowering.

Much of the empowerment comes from doing the work to move through the grieving, including rebuilding and experiencing new relationships. Doing the grief work also helped me to know and accept that Kathy is in a wonderful place.

All along the way, I have had such solid support from family and friends in the form of encouragement and challenge. I also want to share one other element of encouragement that I have been blessed with over these last few years. From time to time, I "hear" from Kathy, both in my work with Johana and also in my dreams and meditations. I want to share her messages to me, as a way to celebrate the gift she continues to be in my life and in the lives of all those she touched. More importantly, it is a way for me to celebrate just how totally good it feels to be where I am today. Where I am today goes way beyond just feeling good . . . it actually feels great, and I know I am so blessed. Doing the grief work helped me to know and accept that Kathy is in a wonderful place. I hope in sharing Kathy's messages that have come to me, it will give you a sense of why feeling blessed is so possible:

July 2017

- Lighten up, have fun, open up and laugh more
- You are such a gift, so be yourself as you start meeting others, there is someone else out there who will become your beloved. I had my turn, and you will find another

- I have other work to do, helping women see themselves more positively and be able to find their joy

August 2017

- We are both connected, and we are free
- I'm giving you a big smile for how you are opening up now

May 2018

- I am so proud of you and who you are and what you are doing in the world
- I am so grateful for our time together
- You are so loved, and I love you so much. I am with you always
- I am the fluffy white flower floating to you in the air
- I am in the breeze that brushes against you, listen for my voice
- I am here and I have your back
- Be adventurous in your life, and your work, and your relationships

October 2019

- Pay attention to finding your way back to the fullness of your true self

- Keep finding understanding to continue the letting-go, while holding-on to what you experienced while we were together as the total acceptance of yourself, just as you are

November 2019

- John, celebrate your growth by cranking-up your music really loud at home! (Which I now love to do very often!)

February 2020

- Johana, I am here to help work on John's heart space
- John, you have to keep doing your work on staying connected to Source (God) and your open-heart place. I am in that state already and don't have that work to do now! (It felt like Kathy was gloating a little bit with that jab!)

March 2020

- I am applauding the fact that you are able to express your excitement about moving forward
- I am especially applauding your finding your own consciousness/energy work, in addition to The Cramer Institute work

Kathy was right. It's true that I have been covering some very important ground for myself and learning a lot along the way. Recognizing that, in this moment I am telling myself to savor every incremental learning, realization, improvement, step forward, new awareness, and knowing—like all of those new levels of awareness that I have been experiencing big time now! All of this combined is creating a very clear sense of empowerment for me.

MY NEWFOUND DEPTH OF UNCONDITIONAL SELF-LOVE

Coming out of the grief work in Lifetime #3.5 and now into this 4th Lifetime, I have been able to get back to feeling a lightness and vibrancy and eagerness for life. I found that eagerness by letting myself experience the feeling of excitement for my own life, even though I didn't know exactly what this new life would mean. And I was able to anchor that eagerness by giving-in to how good it feels to be alive and vibrant and excited and hopeful and happy! I credit this vibrancy to my newfound understanding that I can be living from a place of unconditional love, rather than trying to find it, as if it were not in me.

The mission I have now, in front of me, is to create a world of unconditional love by living fully and courageously from my own open heart. But what does it mean to live fully today?

The answer continues to become clearer:

I know when I stay present, those are truly moments of life lived fully. I know that my challenge is to maintain that for the next moment and then the next and let each moment of presence lead each decision of what is next. I know the challenge is to stay conscious, to keep my focus on what I want and to hold myself in alignment with those desires, knowing that it will happen. If I can stay in my "ice cream place", everything else will take care of itself.

By letting go of outcomes, there comes a detachment that somehow enables my mission to manifest in my life. There is much joy in realizing that what I have been asking for is actually being created.

I know I must pay attention to my thoughts and notice if I am tuned-in to that frequency of unconditional love. I had the lived experience of unconditional love in Lifetime #3 and now my challenge in Lifetime #4 is to hold that feeling in each moment. I have the tools now.

When I can stay in that frequency of love, I will find joy and peace in my life. I can stay there by always loving myself unconditionally. I can make this a choice each day in each moment. I can let myself be at peace and give myself the freedom to love again unconditionally.

I must continually remind myself to speak to that which makes my heart sing. To follow my heart boldly, letting go of any lingering sadness or sorrow. I must do so with no fear and with the courage to live my truth. If I can live in child-like wonder, then joy will find its way into my heart always.

I must always be alert to the question: "What is really going on here?" It invites me to take a step back and maintain a perspective of unconditional love, regardless of what is actually happening.

I must remind myself of the joy that I find in nature and also to ask for help from my Higher Self and my guides. That is a big challenge for me, and I know it's important to forgive myself for any lingering feeling of inadequacy. It's always okay to ask for help. When I can trust that all is well and is just as it should be, then I know I am doing the best that I can.

• • •

I have come to realize that no matter what happens next, I am in a place of true success already in my life—success in how far I have come and success in all that I moved through from the loss of Kathy. I really can say that I am blessed with such abundance in every facet of my current life.

I have found a feeling of aliveness and excitement as I have been exploring new relationships. I have touched the energy that is there for diving-in to a shared life again. Yet with that excitement, I am also realizing the importance of allowing. Allowing things to unfold in a good way. Allowing myself to be deliberate, while at the same time maintaining permission (as former Cardinals baseball announcer Jack Buck would say) to "go crazy folks" and follow my heart.

There is so much more now that is my fourth life. I am past the suffering of loss and now can say that the love of my life is... my life! I realize how critical it was to stay engaged with the grieving process after Kathy's death and now with the creative process of moving forward. It is my self-love coming to bear. It is the experience of unconditional love from and for myself.

Lifetime #4 Perspectives

MY EXPERIENCE OF LOVE

So far, a huge journey of awareness has been my progression, both consciously and unconsciously, through that feeling of "not good enough" to being able to love myself and now knowing the unconditional love for myself I hold within me. More importantly it has been a journey of discovery of what it can be like to actually let this unconditional love shape my experiences in life. Those are the experiences that bring joy, lightness, vibrancy and an eagerness for what's next.

My intention is to keep acknowledging the significance of how far I have come. I want to keep my attention on the flow going forward and be in Wonderland (like Alice!) and enjoy my ongoing exploration--in relationship and alone.

In relationship, I am learning so much more about myself than on my own. I am getting to see the parts of me that I love most. I am also getting to see the parts I want to change most. In relationship, I can share my love in so many ways. I can open to be loved in just as many ways.

Alone I am getting to do my deep dives into self-love, exploring the aspects of myself that have been revealed, most often through relationships. It is a heart-filling dance. It is a very heart-warming place.

As I hold the intention of finding a new primary relationship, I want to see how the new conversations and potential new relationships are a reflection of the work I have been doing on myself. It is important to notice which of them are "effortless" and really pay attention to those. In other words, I believe that the self-love I now hold will enable me to attract a relationship capable of reflecting that love.

MY EVOLUTION IN CONSCIOUSNESS

When I learn and integrate each lesson learned about myself, I take on more self-awareness and that, I believe, elevates my consciousness.

In exploring my level of consciousness so many times earlier in my life, my wondering about an experience has moved to a new awareness, and now it is so often moving from there to conscious knowing. I wonder about an experience I have had, which then brings me a new awareness once I have looked more closely at that experience. Then I am finding a confirmation deep down of this awareness, as if I "knew it" all along. When I slow down enough to allow my knowing to emerge, I find myself trusting that all really is as it should be. I keep experiencing this through the gateway of being present.

Just "staying present" sounds way too simple . . . and at the same time, for me, it is always a challenge to do so and I find it has to be a conscious choice. Looking at all of this helps me to know I want to live my life as a series of conscious choices. And I am so grateful to know that I can consciously choose to live every day in the level of consciousness that I experience as unconditional love.

The learning through my first intimate relationship after Kathy's death was also a chance to see some lessons are harder to learn than others. As a result, it is not guaranteed that once I am able to claim greater self-awareness and higher consciousness that I can continuously live from such a place. That knowing keeps me vigilant in my dance with my ego!

I know I must stay in my place of excitement about the exploration and the possibilities for what's next in all facets of my life. And all the while, be intentional about knowing and creating this vibrational place of unconditional love.

I know I must stay present and hold my vibration at that frequency of unconditional love and allow myself to be in that state, to let go of trying to figure-out everything, which is my clear "default position."

I get to that place of unconditional love by finding the feeling (of love) that I want to experience. I remember a time when I was in that vibrational feeling, dwell on that, then move into a deeper experience of just that feeling (vibration) and try to consciously hold that for the rest of my day.

And maybe as the ultimate reminder for myself, I must keep finding more ways to simply have fun! After all, being in my "ice cream place" is a great excuse to enjoy some actual ice cream (with chocolate sauce)!

A MOMENT TO REFLECT . . . ON LIFETIME #4

THIS 4TH LIFE HAS a huge element of (re)birth attached to it. It is a time of coming back to myself. It is a time of truly coming alive!

It is also a time of learning about and ultimately knowing so much more about the many facets that make-up who I am. It is a time for connecting with each of those facets and having fun recombining or trying new combinations for myself. There is a playfulness that presents itself here and my job is to fully embrace that playfulness.

This playfulness certainly contributes to the lightness of spirit that is so often present for me. That lightness is also a product of holding the vibrational frequency of unconditional love. That is truly a felt experience within my body that is becoming more familiar each day. It is a compelling place and one that I aspire to live with continuously. (And I know I am still human!)

This represents an entirely new place of understanding for me—both an understanding of my "human dance" and that of my "soul dance". I have found my way, so far, through the labyrinth that is my life. I have found that I have had what I needed in order to do so. I know I was able to do this by trusting myself, each step along the way.

This now helps me extend my personal experience and hold the belief that we can each find our way through the labyrinth of our lives, that we have what we need to do so if we will trust ourselves each step along the way.

Giving myself all these moments to reflect on each of my lifetimes has helped me maintain perspective and be able to savor all the gifts that have brought me to this point. It helps me see the importance of trusting my own process - even when I have no idea what "my process" really is. And it helps me take yet another step in defining and then experiencing this amazing 4th Life as it happens each day.

Original heartwork by Jaxon Wesley Davis - ©2021

• CONCLUSION •

Holding Our Lives with Open Hands

WHAT IS IT THAT IS WAITING TO BREAK OPEN IN YOU?

Just when I feel sure my waking-up to the unconditional love within me has reached the pinnacle for this lifetime, I am reminded there is always so much more. In fact, I can look back at my first three lifetimes and find many places where I would have said, "Now this is it!" And then, yet one more layer of the onion is peeled back or one new turn in the labyrinth of my life is discovered. I do know each step comes in its "Divine time" and that keeps sending me back to the realization that I am not really in charge here!

And it causes me to wonder: If all of these lifetimes in my journey have been about my breaking open to new heights and new depths of who I am, can the same be true for others? I know I am not unique in any particular way, relative to my abilities or capability. My journey so far has been one of an ordinary person finding an extraordinary path, one of unconditional love and continually expanding consciousness. This path has allowed me to find my trust in myself, with much help along the way, and it has opened me to find so many new places of understanding who I am.

Now in my 4th Lifetime, my journey is bringing me more clarity around the need for us to collectively develop a higher state of consciousness. This starts first with me and then with each of us being able to accept—even embrace or dare I say it, love—our differences. It means suspending judgment of each other, especially around our beliefs and our religions. It means being able to accept another person just for who they are.

Accepting others, especially those different from us, became truly possible for me when I realized we are all connected at a spiritual level–the level where we all have that same spark of the Divine within us. We are all the same at the soul level, at our Essence. At our Essence, we are Unconditional Love. I believe that when we each can find this understanding, we will start to treat each other with compassion, with care and tolerance. And I believe when we are able to do that, we will find a world where it is possible to have a completely different experience, one of unconditional love, for each and all of us.

What if we could each just love ourselves unconditionally? Wouldn't the rest of it follow from there?

What is it that is waiting to break open in each of us in order to live in this place of unconditional love?

WHAT CAN I DO TO HELP US ALL BE IN UNCONDITIONAL LOVE?

THAT REMAINS A REALLY big question and is still a very daunting task, one that clearly has no easy answer. The more I have pondered on it, the more I keep seeing I must approach this through how I show up in my world every day. I see that it means two things for me:

1) How I choose to BE in the world, and

2) How I choose to engage with others through my work and my on-going personal relations, as well as my chance encounters along the way.

That realization creates the conditions that help me shift in a number of ways. I have become more conscious of loving myself and others with unconditional love. I have become more aware of my judgments of others and of my own intolerance around beliefs different from mine and what I need to do to shift away from those judgments.

In my work, I challenge myself to help the individuals and groups I work with, to become more aware of themselves. I help someone see something in themselves they had not seen before or help them discover a new asset, strength or capability about themselves (or their team) they had not realized up to then. As I take these steps, I know I am helping raise their consciousness, at least in a small way. I believe that those small steps open to even larger shifts, as awareness grows and beliefs about self expand.

This entire path of discovery around my desire to see us living together from a place of higher consciousness has clarified a central theme and vision for my life, a vision that feels even more critical at this time in my life. As I find more ways to share about my experiences and the beliefs they create, it brings greater clarity to how my life has brought me to this point and more importantly, how it can carry me forward from here.

I trust that sharing how my experiences with unconditional love have shaped me can offer some guidance for shifting our collective consciousness. I trust that opening up about my own evolution of consciousness can help make it possible to see and sense a world actually filled with unconditional love.

I know this is what the world needs, because when I say that, it feels like a basic truth–at least for me. I can feel it in my bones, and I can tell that my understanding is expanding. The infinite and eternal love of Source is within me, as it is in all of us and it feels like it wants to come out. It wants to come out and play. It wants to create, and it wants to bring others to that realization–that this same unconditional love exists inside of them and all of us as well.

It is my mission to find ways to make this possible, to find a clear strong voice for this possibility, to encourage, help, and guide others to find their versions of a world of unconditional love. This is what I will be spending my time on, using my voice for, writing my words about and living my life as. This mission is why this book exists.

My mission—and my key challenge—is to find the bridge from where we are today to some version of this new world I keep envisioning.

I know what the buzz and vibration of this new world feels like inside of me. There is an excitement to simply be alive now and to be alive in this particular way. It is this excitement that now lets me love, know and appreciate the life I had with Kathy and yet not be swallowed up any longer or held in a negative way by the grief of losing her and the life we had together. It is the excitement of living fully.

WHAT DOES IT MEAN TO LIVE MY LIFE FULLY?

I ANSWER THIS QUESTION at one level through my intention and then by my action of being fully present in each moment. I extend the living of it by being deliberate and conscious about the things I choose to do each day. Is this next thing I am considering life-giving to me? Is it a way I will be living fully? These questions help me create my version of a world that knows unconditional love.

I am eager to see what I do next and what support I will find along the way. I know that whatever I do, I will get something good out of it. I want to be sure and stay awake, stay conscious because that's when very good things happen. I will pay attention and embrace it all and everything will be as it should be, as I continue forward on this fourth life journey.

Follow the flow, follow the ease, follow my feelings. I know it's going to get easier, even effortless. It's going to get better and I'll have a lot of fun on the ride ahead.

A Moment (or two) for a Final Reflection

In one of the workshops we do at The Cramer Institute,[15] we take individuals and groups through a process of discovering and looking at their own "heroic journeys". The classic story arc of the heroic journey has six phases that are common for all such stories, including: The Call for a significant change; The Resistance to being the one leading the change; The Threshold Crossing, when a commitment is made to go forward; The Journey, where progress is made and challenges are faced; The Supreme Ordeal, the one challenge that could derail everything; and The Return Home, where a new world is found and celebrated.

In the workshops, the heroic journey exercise is a way for participants to gain understanding and perspective, as well as appreciate the life they are living. Without realizing it at the onset, this writing process has offered me the chance to see The Heroic Journey of My Lifetime!

15 https://cramerinstitute.com

In my lifetimes of my journey, I could succinctly describe "My Call" as that deep desire to help in shifting collective consciousness, such that the experience is unconditional love. Clearly "My Resistance" to that call came with the question: Who am I to be able to cause the collective consciousness to shift?

"My Threshold Crossing" was when I said to myself: But wait, I can work on my own level of consciousness. I can create a world of unconditional love by living fully and courageously from my own open heart. I can hold the intention to live my life every day in the level of consciousness that is an experience of unconditional love.

I now believe that "My Journey" has evolved around that intention, both at an unconscious level early on and now in a very conscious way. Each discussion and reflection in Lifetimes 1, 2, and 3 speak to the contribution to this (unknowing) journey of consciousness - until it was known. The journey through each lifetime so far has helped me get to where I am today.

I can truly say that for me "The Supreme Ordeal" I have experienced (so far) has been my Lifetime 3.5. Journeying through the depths of loss and finding myself anew along the way, has in turn set me up for quite the glorious "Return Home". That is what I now see is happening as my experience so far in Lifetime 4. Having and knowing my "ice cream place" alone has made it an amazing new place to be. Holding the excitement for what's coming, the same as when I sat at the top of the stairs on Christmas morning as a child, lets me feel myself coming alive every day in this new 4th Life.

It has also let me find yet one more new aspiration for myself as this 4th Lifetime continues . . . I speak to that in the epilogue. However, before going there, let me step way back from this journey for a moment and remind myself of several key tenets that I want to take with me each day:

Never stop loving myself.
Seek awareness.

Never stop loving my life.
Make my choices deliberately and consciously.

Always extend my love to others.
Trust in my sense of knowing.

Always open to the love coming to me.
Stay awake and present.

Original heartwork by Jaxon Wesley Davis - ©2021

• EPILOGUE •

The Generations of My Lifetime

UNCONDITIONAL LOVE WITH MY KIDS, GRANDKIDS, AND NOW A GREAT GRANDKID

TWO DAYS BEFORE MY 70th birthday I got to meet and hold my great granddaughter, Lillith Danielle. She was just 6 weeks old at that point. Yes, I agree with everyone who has already told me: "you are too young to be a great grandfather!" And my response is always the same: "I didn't have much say in the matter!"

The moment I held Lilly in my arms was a moment of pure grace. I was physically embracing her with such clear unconditional love and unconditional love was looking right back at me through her dark blue eyes.

My granddaughter Nadianna was twenty-one when Lilly was born. She is my daughter Emily's only child.

Nadianna was radiant in the pride she holds for her daughter, clear about her responsibilities as a new mom and showing a sense of maturity that was actually not surprising to me. Her own childhood had brought her to an early maturity, way beyond her years, that has served her well . . . and is bringing a sense of calm confidence in her early days as a mom.

I went from Nadianna's to my son Adam's home to spend time with his kids, my three other grandchildren. The two boys, Jaden (fifteen) and Jaxon (twelve), were consumed in sports stuff. Jaden is the traditional sports jock and is a straight-A high school freshman. He is making a run at baseball and football. Jax is the "e-sports" jock and a budding young artist and musician. He loves gaming competitions, both as a player and a spectator. It's a whole new world I barely know anything about at this point. Rosemary (twenty) is already an accomplished artist and is in a "gap year" contemplating what her next steps around college will be, while working restaurant jobs to earn some money.

I am blessed beyond measure with these next generation kids in my life. I am even more blessed by my two children, Adam and Emily, and the place they hold in my life. They are both so close in my heart and so dear as supporters, advocates, counselors, and challengers. They love me beyond measure, they push me to keep finding my best self and they stand with me no matter what. The love has always been there but we have worked hard to have the kind of loving relationships we enjoy today.

If I had to headline my journey of unconditional love with myself and these next three generations, it would be something like this:

For me:
I had it–I lost it–I found that it was in me all along

For my (two) children:
I gave it–I took it away–I found it was there all along

For my (four) grandchildren:
I gave it–I gave it some more–I find it is always there

For my (one) great granddaughter:
I am giving it–I am giving it more frequently–I find it is always there

I will try to fill in the story of what I mean by these headlines in what follows. I'll pick up with where I left off talking about Lilly, the six-week-old.

Original artwork by Rosemary Renee' Davis - ©2021

MY GREAT GRANDDAUGHTER: LILLITH DANIELLE

TAKING THAT FRAGILE SIX-WEEK-OLD baby into my arms was indeed a moment of unconditional love. How could it not be? I was giving it freely and I was getting it just as freely. Big bright eyes, chubby cheeks pushed out from her small, but huge smile and the softest skin all combined to melt my heart. Holding her as she kept flailing around with her arms and legs, I tried to get her to find a grip on my finger. Her little hand could not yet wrap itself completely around my index finger. Yet when she held on, it was with a momentary grip of strength. My love was and will flow unconditionally for this precious little girl!

Nadianna was clearly overjoyed to have Lilly here. She told me more about the three "false alarms" that sent them to the ER thinking delivery was imminent. She described how Lilly's father, Tristan, had started insisting weeks before that Nadia should have her hospital bag at the ready. They added a couple of more things to it each time they returned from those three ER visits and were quite ready when the actual moment of "this is it" labor presented itself.

What was most thrilling to me was how both Tristan and Nadianna are embracing parenthood. This child will not be lacking from a loving home and a very attentive dad and mom. She will not be lacking from loving grandparents and great grandparents. And for me, the question that pops into my head each time I meet a newborn is, what is it you have come to be and do in this world?

I do know Lillith is now embarking on her "one wild and precious life." I know she is bringing a precious new chapter to her parents' lives—who I think would be quick to say how wild it is already becoming. And it causes me to think back to those early months of first becoming a father myself and it helps me realize how the time has flown by and how I do hold each moment as so precious. Especially now, as I consider all the love that both my children have brought - and are bringing - into my life.

Back to the question of what Lillith might be here to be and do . . . I'm going to go out on a limb here and share one answer to that question that came to me before Lillith was born. In the previous chapter titled "My Open-Heart Journey", I shared that in my sessions with spiritual-healer Johana, Kathy will often visit to deliver a message of motivation or encouragement that I might find beneficial at the time.

So I was having a session with Johana and Kathy came in spirit. The message she brought me was to keep holding the place of joy in my life I was finding so clearly, and at the same time to be aware of the emotions of others–especially family–and not let that bring me down. Acknowledge where they are yet hold my place of joy in a way that allows me to be fully present with them. Given that I had a Thanksgiving trip planned to be with my family, that message seemed quite timely, even though I had no idea how it would exactly apply. It did apply, as I found out during my visit, to things that were stirring with my son and his family. It also applied to much of what I was seeing with Nadianna, as she was in her seventh month of pregnancy

What happened next in that session with Johana is the point in bringing it up here. As soon as Kathy had shared her message through Johana, a very surprising thing happened next. Johana asked me if someone in the family was expecting a baby, I said yes, my granddaughter is pregnant with Lillith Danielle. (They chose Danielle as her middle name after Kathy who has the same middle name!) Johana then said, well Lillith has also joined us here in spirit!

Lillith was there in spirit to say that she wanted her parents to know: Her favorite color is purple! She is coming to be your daughter to be able to teach you about patience. She has chosen Nadianna as her mom because she is so strong. She knows Nadia's life has enabled her to gain so much strength as a woman and as a person. Lillith wanted them to know there is nothing to worry about and that she knows you get stressed when you worry and when you do it takes you away from being the loving people you are. So stop worrying, especially because you have nothing to prove to anyone else. Trust yourselves and remember the self-confidence you have and never doubt yourself . . . trust, trust, trust. And remember, my favorite color is purple!

I was in tears by the time this message was completed. The experience of connecting in this way at that time was so overwhelmingly unexpected. It felt like such a huge gift and a very reverent privilege to hear these words from a great granddaughter, yet to join us in the physical world. I wrote out the message in a letter to Nadianna and Tristan and gave it to them during my visit the next week. I had also found a collection of purple baby stuff that I presented in a purple gift bag!

Delivering this message to the (un)expecting parents was itself an experience of unconditional love. As I watched both their eyes swell with tears, I knew they were about to begin a truly amazing new chapter in their lives. Feeling Lillith's little hand find its grip on my finger cemented the connection that started that day in the session with Johana. That connection allowed the love to flow unconditionally in that moment . . . and it let me know it will always be there for her. I also know I can hardly wait to take her shopping someday and see what color the outfit will be that she lets me buy for her.

I love you Lillith.

With all my heart.

MY GRANDCHILDREN: NADIANNA KAI, ROSEMARY RENEE', JADEN MATEO, AND JAXON WESLEY

I HAVE CERTAINLY BOUGHT these four lovely grandkids in my life outfits of all kinds over the last twenty+ years. Lately, however, it is all about gift cards so they can go shopping on their own without having to bring Papaw John along. I did see that one coming as they grew older, and I still love them completely!

Becoming a grandparent has been a sacred journey for me. As I discussed in Lifetime #1, my maternal grandfather was a huge influence in my life. I carry his unconditional love with me every day and I aspire to create a similar experience with my own grandchildren. I get to stay connected with my grandchildren in a much more frequent way than I ever did with my grandparents . . . through the technology of texting! I am texting with one or more of them each week. Yes, there are (rare) times when we actually do a phone call, however it is usually when I get tired of typing out what would be much easier (for me) to simply speak out loud directly to them. Each exchange always ends with a "I love you", to and from them. I may have heard that from my grandparents once or twice each year when visiting them over a holiday or summer break. They meant it just as much as I do, but just couldn't deliver that message as often as I get to with my grandchildren.

I have come to believe I can't deliver that 'I love you' message enough. I long for them to know that and to hear it directly from me. I feel it for them all the time– my heart is full of loving them–loving them, yes, unconditionally. Of course, I flinch at some of the choices they are making along the way and when they ask or seem open, I will offer my perspective. I know however, that they are in their own journeys and perhaps the best way I can support them is in just being sure they know I am there for them.

In the months after Kathy died, I found myself reaching out to each one of them directly to hold them and let them "hold me". I brought the boys to visit me over a long weekend and we took-in some Cardinal baseball games. I flew each of the girls separately to be with me as well during that time. Sharing that time together was of course very precious, sharing some of our grieving together it felt like was also needed.

The boys have come back each summer for baseball games, fishing and just hanging out together. As the girls grew older, somehow my time with them was replaced by time with boyfriends! Still, the texting and visits continue as we each work the other into our schedules. I always want to find more time and yet I know they are finding their own lives.

As I mentioned earlier, they are each unique and coming into their own in their own ways. Nadianna is in school working on a business degree, while working almost full time and now adding being a mother on top of all of that. Rose is sorting through options to define the next phase of her life as a budding young adult. The two boys are immersed in their own worlds of middle school and high school, as they should be at his stage.

And all the time Papaw John stands watching them, being with them in spirit, in person and by text. I hold them close in my heart. I send them my love directly and indirectly each day. I let them know I am here to support them in the best ways I can. I keep loving them unconditionally and then I do it some more. I trust that my deep desire to be an example for them, as my grandfather was for me, is playing out in some way that will serve them well in their lives. I trust that they will always know how important they are to me.

I love you Nadianna.

I love you Rosemary.

I love you Jaden.

I love you Jaxon.

Each and all, I love you with all my heart.

MY CHILDREN: ADAM WESLEY AND EMILY RENEE'

THE LOVE FOR MY grandchildren is a reflection of the love I have for my children. It is a reflection of the love they both have for their kids. Adam and Emily will each tell you that their children mean more to them than anything. I can say the same thing about the two of them. Yet, it is through the many ups and downs of my own parenthood that I have been able to get so clear about the gift of having my two children in my life.

Today and every day now in my life, I try to 100% love Adam and Emily for who they are in their own lives at any moment in time. There is clarity in that expression of my unconditional love for them. There is strength in that love that has grown and evolved over the last forty+ years they have been with me. There have been rough spots along the way. Times where I know they were experiencing my love as very conditional. That is why I say I gave it and I took it away—and that I found I have had an unconditional love in my heart for them all along. Today it gets expressed in many ways at many times. It took some work along the way to find this place.

I talked about some of their childhood in Lifetime #2. As they were children, my love certainly did flow unconditionally for each of them. We will always point to the games of "tickle-tackle" as a great expression of the fun together and the love we held for each other. Born 15 months apart, they grew up together and were always best of friends or occasionally worst of enemies.

While there are many important and loving memories created during their formative years, I do think they would each say that I was an absent father along the way a lot of times. As I mentioned, there was a lot of travel away when I began to build my career. Our connection was always there, and the missed opportunities were plentiful as well. We created some unbelievable times while living overseas and that served to deepen the bonds that were present at that time during our lives.

As they both moved into their teenage years, those bonds became strained and were even broken in their own ways at times. In talking with them recently about this writing project, we touched on some of those hard times. I remembered the moment that my love for Adam showed up in its most conditional form. It was the night I lost it with him over my expectations of his needing to do better in his math class. My frustration and anger raged in a moment I will never forget. I literally saw Adam's spirit break right in front of me . . . because of me and my harsh words. I knew in that moment I had lost him in an irreparable way.

That loss turned into a physical separation when he dropped out of high school and became a road kid for several years, trying to find himself after my separation with his mom. And it took years to work my (and our) way back into the loving, trusting relationship that we enjoy today. In the last several years, Adam has had his own version of a spiritual awakening and I am witnessing his life path open in some amazing new ways. It has been a huge blessing to be able to see, hear and share the depth of what that is bringing into his life and our relationship.

With Emily, things got really muddled up when her mom and I separated then divorced. To me she seemed to get lost in the shuffle. She was left fending for herself in many ways. She graduated after a rocky finish to high school and then joined her brother on the road. I know my love must have felt very conditional when she announced a year or so later at twenty years old, that she was pregnant. It "wasn't supposed to be that way" in my version of life.

Things shifted when I got to hold Nadianna, then as my first grandchild. The troubled love dissolved in the moment I became a grandfather. Still the course I set to support her, in what eventually became her life as a single mom, put a hidden strain on our relationship. As I was to painfully learn years later in a family counseling session, I became Emily's greatest enabler. My good intentions to help her as she struggled to raise her daughter actually were holding her back and not letting her find her own way to make it in the world.

Emily's world crashed-in on her eventually. She took time off for herself to heal and Nadianna came to live with Kathy and me. She was twelve and just starting middle school. We helped her get started in a new school, set-up one of the spare bedrooms for her and went to work creating a new home life to support her in the best way we could as her mom was away. Kathy and I had been together over fifteen years at that point, and we too were having a big new experience as grandparents—and I would have to say as parents also. We both grew so much closer with Nadianna through that experience, especially Kathy and Nadianna.

That was also the year that my relationship with Emily came to life in its most healthy way and is what has led us to the deep love we share with each other today. The family counseling that came later that year was instrumental for me as I mentioned. I was able to let go and simply start trusting that Emily had the wherewithal to find her own way. It felt like we were both able to start being completely honest and open with each other. I began to see a much healthier and self-reliant young woman emerge after that year of hard personal growth work and my heart opened even more than I could have ever imagined. Emily too has deepened her path of spiritual development, and as with Adam, she and I are sharing many new levels of soul-work with each other.

I love Adam and Emily unconditionally. I am so clear about that–I trust they each know that as well. I relish the time I get with each of them and always want more. I love the depth of the sharing and conversations we have today. I honor the trust we have in each other and the deep will to be there for the other. I smile every time I get a text message from one of them. I often scratch my head when I get Adam's latest suggestion on some new music and wonder where the hell he finds the tunes he sends! Emily now lives close enough that we actually get to spend time together. I especially like the times when she will show up and we can cook a meal together.

While each of my children are very busy living and creating their own lives, we are connected in a deep, real, and poignant way. I know their love for me. I hear it, I feel it and I cherish it. For them I try to be just as clear about my love for them. It is an unconditional love that I have always had for them, hidden though it may have been at times. It is out in the open and thriving now beyond my wildest imagination.

I love you Adam.

I love you Emily.

With all my heart.

A NEW ASPIRATION

As I let the significance of my family experience really sink-in and as my written words linger a little longer, I feel like this "epilogue" may actually be pointing to something more like a "prologue" for what's next.

I discussed earlier, that when I fully embraced being able to create a new life - my Lifetime #4 - I started by setting intentions in each critical dimension of the life I want to now be living. Having now taken the time to touch on my experience with unconditional love as it relates to my family, I want to go back to what I said about relationships:

I choose being present and authentic in all my relationships.

As I look at that intention now through the lens of the "generations of my lifetime", it feels like it falls way too short of what I could actually be - and want to be - creating for this dimension of my new life.

As a new great grandparent, I so readily see and experience Lillith through the eyes of unconditional love. She is pure innocence and with that, pure joy. (Yes, of course, I am not the one changing diapers and up feeding her in the middle of the night!) Yet, how can I bring my unconditional love to her, as she starts her childhood, in a way that supports letting her world expand into all that will be possible for her?

As a grandparent of two teenage boys and now a couple of twenty-something young women, I see their lives being shaped in pivotal developmental moments of their own making. I hold each of these kids in such a deep love from all the time shared so far in their growing-up. How can I show them the world of unconditional love that I believe they can be a part of now . . . if they have that awareness?

As a parent of my two beautiful adult children—both with an ever-deepening spiritual awareness—I have returned to a conscious state of loving them unconditionally. I have learned so much along the way from and with them. I have seen the gap of shattered trust and experienced the healing found in rebuilding. I hold each of our relationships in my very open heart as we continue to grow with each other everyday. How do I find even more ways to open to them and learn with them about a shared world of evolving consciousness and unconditional love?

Seeing some new clarity with these three "generational questions", they point me to an aspirational opportunity I see for myself going forward. What if I can hold each of the questions so clearly, that I find my answers for them in each encounter with each generation? What if I can help them each know the importance of the questions to me, by helping them know the answers as a lived experience with me? What if I can help them know it is possible to live every day in the experience of unconditional love?

Imagine what that world might be like!

I can ... and I am!

Original heartwork by Jaxon Wesley Davis - ©2021

I believe I was quite clear on the gift my children and their children are in my life . . . and I am saying a simple thank you, Adam and Emily, for your on-going love, each day.

As has been noted throughout, the artwork included in this book was commissioned work by my two grandchildren, Rosemary and Jaxon. I am so thankful for their work and very proud of their contribution to this project. I am thrilled at all of their artistic expressions and will always be grateful for their joyful participation in creating this book

I have a huge thank you to and a most heart-felt appreciation for Danielle Goodman[16], who served as my developmental editor and trusted guide in this entire writing project. I have known Danielle and her work for years now and it was a true privilege to get to do this book with her. She has been instrumental in helping craft a cohesive and focused finished product from the volumes of journal notes, cards, and personal writing I brought to the table. Her joy and exuberance were

16 http://www.daniellegoodman.me

always there and served as continuous encouragement for me.

The writing I included in Lifetime #3 between me and Kathy was a small sample of what was available from all the cards and letters we exchanged. Jean Fenwick took on the task of transcribing those hundreds of greeting cards to provide an electronic copy to use in this project. Jean was so meticulous in recording the words, the formatting and the beauty within all of those exchanges. I am forever grateful for Jean's contribution to this project.

I shared much about the work I have been doing with Johana Probst and want to end by saying that her guidance and clarity continue to be a source of strength and understanding everyday in my life.

Barbara T. you are a refuge and shining light for me now and always. I get it on so many levels why we decided to be brother and sister in this amazing lifetime together. Susan and Tim, I feel your love so clearly every time we get to be together.

Jan, Pat, Jamie, Andy, Karina and Ali, thank you for loving me in all the ways you do and holding a place of family that is such a treasure. Deanna and Stephen thank you for how you have made it possible to circle back and be a part of each others' lives in such a loving and caring way.

My heartfelt gratitude goes out to Julie, Joe, Tina, Max, Ann and Bill for their constant support, encouragement and enduring friendship.

JuLee Brand and her W. Brand Publishing[17] Team have been amazing to work with in the publishing phase of this project. I quickly found out it was a "hang on for the ride" experience once we got started! JuLee has an energy and enthusiasm for what she does that is so wonderfully contagious. And she knows how to get the job done in a really fun and efficient manner.

Mary Ann, Beth, Chris, Jeremy, Eric, Eliot and the entire team at Big Wide Sky[18] are not only dear friends, they are the consummate professionals in all they do. Their expertise in branding, website development and marketing have been invaluable. Most importantly for me has been their constant encouragement each step along the way. Thank you for believing in me and taking on this new topic area the book has offered.

17 https://www.wbrandpub.com
18 https://bigwidesky.com

I also want to say a special thank you to Becky Robinson, founder of Weaving Influence[19], for her generous guidance and heart-felt support of her team, including Wendy, Christy and Megan in the final stages of this project. I am very grateful Becky for your willingness to work with me, even while finishing your own book.

I have made specific mention of a number of the women and men in my life that have been and continue to be a beautiful part of my life journey. There are other close friends and colleagues not mentioned that are always there for me and have been through the highs and lows with support, love and encouragement. Sharon, Dale, Laura, Mike, Pam, Kelly, Laura L.H. and Judy, along with Sheldon, Harry, Mike, Phil, Bob, Robyn, David, Kurt, Hugh, Barry and Dick. Thank you from the depth of my heart for being in my life in every way that you are.

And finally, I want to acknowledge my most loyal and faithful 4th Life companion, Sophie Tucker. She is my cute little fifteen-year-old Bichon Friese puppy and she never leaves my side while we are together in the house. She is the penultimate expression of unconditional love.

---

19 https://weavinginfluence.com

John S. Davis

JOHN DAVIS IS THE Managing Partner at The Cramer Institute. John is a sought-after executive coach, workshop facilitator and corporate consultant. He is especially skillful in moving individuals and groups to new levels of performance and effectiveness, particularly during times that require organizational change and transformation. With leaders, John's coaching targets excellence in self-awareness, communication, influence, team building and conflict resolution skills.

In addition, John designs and leads training for The Cramer Institute on mindset management using Asset-Based Thinking® (ABT), Lead Positive®[20] coaching and workshops for individual and team leadership

---

20 https://cramerinstitute.com/lead-positive/

development, as well as ABT communication, through Power & Presence coaching.

John joined The Cramer Institute in 2006 after a distinguished 31-year career in manufacturing operations, strategic planning, change management and organizational development.

In his community work, John contributes his one-on-one coaching and group leadership by serving on training staffs for the Mankind Project (MKP), an international non-profit organization for men focused on personal growth and leadership development.

John has served as an adjunct staff member for the Center of Creative Arts (COCA)[21] in St. Louis, where he facilitated workshops for the COCAbiz programs, bringing an experience of the arts into organizations to foster creativity and innovation. John also works with other non-profit organizations and with College Bound in St. Louis[22] helping youth and young adults develop as leaders.

John holds Bachelor's and Master's degrees in Mechanical Engineering from Oklahoma State University and an MBA from Southern Illinois University.

www.johndavisjourneys.com

---

21 https://www.cocastl.org

22 https://www.collegeboundstl.org

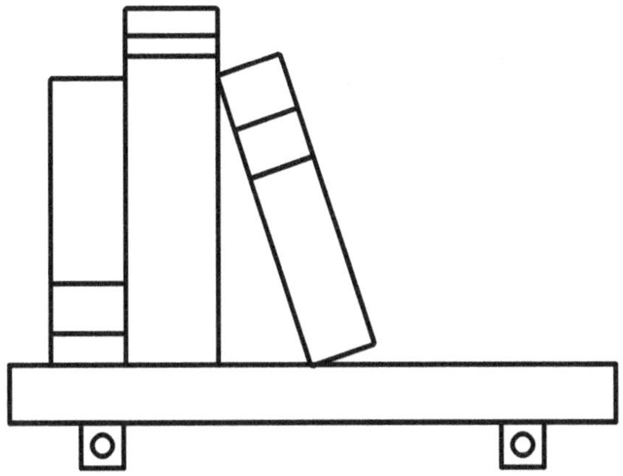

Like this book?

Consider sharing it with others!

- Share or mention the book on social media platforms. Use the hashtag **#LifetimesOfaJourney**
- Write a book review on Amazon, GoodReads, or other review sites
- Learn more about John's transformational coaching and workshop process called **"Ready For What's Next" at www.johndavisjourneys.com**
- Pick up a copy for your friends and family
- Sign up to receive blog posts and email updates at www.johndavisjourneys.com
- Follow W. Brand Publishing on Twitter, Instagram, and FaceBook **@wbrandpub www.wbrandpub.com**

CPSIA information can be obtained
at www.ICGtesting.com
Printed in the USA
BVHW030726251021
619812BV00014B/536/J